WORKSHOPS THAT WORK

100 ideas to make your training ev

Latest titles in the McGraw-Hill Training Series

DESIGNING AND ACHIEVING COMPETENCY
A Competency Based Approach to Developing People and
Organizations
Editors: Rosemary Boam
and Paul Sparrow   ISBN 0-07-707572-2

TOTAL QUALITY TRAINING
The Quality Culture and Quality Trainer
Brian Thomas   ISBN 0-07-707472-6

CAREER DEVELOPMENT AND PLANNING
A Guide for Managers, Trainers and Personnel Staff
Malcolm Peel   ISBN 0-07-707554-4

SALES TRAINING
A Guide to Developing Effective Salespeople
Frank S Salisbury   ISBN 0-07-707458-0

CLIENT-CENTRED CONSULTING
A Practical Guide for Internal Advisers and Trainers
Peter Cockman, Bill Evans
and Peter Reynolds   ISBN 0-07-707685-0

TRAINING TO MEET THE TECHNOLOGY CHALLENGE
Trevor Bentley   ISBN 0-07-707589-7

IMAGINATIVE EVENTS Volumes I & II
Ken Jones   ISBN 0-07-707679-6 Volume I
              ISBN 0-07-707680-X Volume II
              ISBN 0-07-707681-8 for set of Volume I & II

LEARNING THROUGH SIMULATIONS
A Guide to the Design and Use of Simulations in Business and Education
John Fripp   ISBN 0-07-707588-9

MEETINGS MANAGEMENT
Leslie Rae   ISBN 0-07-707782-2

TRAINING FOR PROFIT
Philip Darling   ISBN 0-07-707785-7

Details of these and other titles in the series are available from:

The Product Manager, Professional Books, McGraw-Hill Book Company Europe,
Shoppenhangers Road, Maidenhead, Berkshire, SL6 2QL, United Kingdom.
Telephone: 0628 23432 Fax: 0628 770224

Workshops that work

100 ideas to make your training events more effective

Tom Bourner, Vivien Martin and Phil Race

McGRAW-HILL BOOK COMPANY

London · New York · St Louis · San Francisco · Auckland
Bogotá · Caracas · Lisbon · Madrid · Mexico · Milan
Montreal · New Delhi · Panama · Paris · San Juan · São Paulo
Singapore · Sydney · Tokyo · Toronto

Published by
McGRAW-HILL Book Company Europe
Shoppenhangers Road, Maidenhead, Berkshire, SL6 2QL, England.
Telephone: 0628 23432
Fax: 0628 770224

British Library Cataloguing in Publication Data
Bourner, Tom
   Workshops That Work: 100 Ideas to Make
   Your Training Events More Effective.—
   (McGraw-Hill Training Series)
   I. Title   II. Series
   658.3

   ISBN 0-07-707800-4

Library of Congress Cataloging-in-Publication Data
Bourner, Tom,
   Workshops that work: 100 ideas to make your training events more
effective/Tom Bourner, Viv Martin, and Phil Race.
      p.   cm. — (McGraw-Hill training series)
   Includes bibliographical references and index.
   ISBN 0-07-707800-4
   1. Employees—Training of. 2. Workshops (Adult education).
I. Martin, Viv, II. Race, Philip. III. Title.
IV. Series.
   HF5549.5.T7B596   1993
   658.3'124—dc20   92–46626
                                                           CIP

1234 CL 9543

Typeset by Book Ens Limited, Baldock, Herts
Printed and bound in Great Britain by Clays Ltd, St Ives plc

Contents

* Key (when to use): Before a workshop (Before); at the start (Start); during a workshop (During); at the end (End); after a workshop (After); anytime (Anytime)

*** Key (when to use):** *Before a workshop (Before); at the start (Start); during a workshop (During); at the end (End); after a workshop (After); anytime (Anytime)*

*** Key (when to use):** Before a workshop (Before); at the start (Start); during a workshop (During); at the end (End); after a workshop (After); anytime (Anytime)*

** **Key (when to use):** Before a workshop (Before); at the start (Start); during a workshop (During); at the end (End); after a workshop (After); anytime (Anytime)*

* *Key (when to use): Before a workshop (Before); at the start (Start); during a workshop (During); at the end (End); after a workshop (After); anytime (Anytime)*

*** Key (when to use):** *Before a workshop (Before); at the start (Start); during a workshop (During); at the end (End); after a workshop (After); anytime (Anytime)*

Series preface

Training and development are now firmly centre stage in most organizations, if not all. Nothing unusual in that—for some organizations. They have always seen training and development as part of the heart of their businesses—but more and more must see that same way.

The demographic trends through the 1990s will inject into the marketplace severe competition for good people who will need good training. Young people without conventional qualifications, skilled workers in redundant crafts, people out of work, women wishing to return to work—all will require excellent training to fit them to meet the job demands of the 1990s and beyond.

But excellent training does not spring from what we have done well in the past. T&D specialists are in a new ball game. 'Maintenance' training—training to keep up skill levels to do what we have always done—will be less in demand. Rather, organization, work and market change training are now much more important and will remain so for some time. Changing organizations and people is no easy task, requiring special skills and expertise which, sadly, many T&D specialists do not possess.

To work as a 'change' specialist requires us to get to centre stage—to the heart of the company's business. This means we have to ask about future goals and strategies and even be involved in their development, at least as far as T&D policies are concerned.

This demands excellent communication skills, political expertise, negotiating ability, diagnostic skills—indeed, all the skills a good internal consultant requires.

The implications for T&D specialists are considerable. It is not enough merely to be skilled in the basics of training, we must also begin to act like business people and to think in business terms and talk the language of business. We must be able to resource training not just from within but by using the vast array of external resources. We must be able to manage our activities as well as any other manager. We must share in the creation and communication of the company's vision. We must never let the goals of the company out of our sight.

In short, we may have to grow and change with the business. It will be hard. We shall have to demonstrate not only relevance but also value for money and achievement of results. We shall be our own boss, as accountable for results as any other line manager, and we shall have to deal with fewer internal resources.

The challenge is on, as many T&D specialists have demonstrated to me over the past few years. We need to be capable of meeting that challenge. This is why McGraw-Hill Book Company Europe have planned and launched this major new training series—to help us meet that challenge.

The series covers all aspects of T&D and provides the knowledge base from which we can develop plans to meet the challenge. They are practical books for the professional person. They are a starting point for planning our journey into the twenty-first century.

Use them well. Don't just read them. Highlight key ideas, thoughts, action pointers or whatever, and have a go at doing something with them. Through experimentation we evolve; through stagnation we die.

I know that all the authors in the McGraw-Hill Training Series would want me to wish you good luck. Have a great journey into the twenty-first century.

ROGER BENNETT
Series Editor

About the series editor

Roger Bennett has over 20 years' experience in training, management education, research and consulting. He has long been involved with trainer training and trainer effectiveness. He has carried out research into trainer effectiveness and conducted workshops, seminars and conferences on the subject around the world. He has written extensively on the subject including the book *Improving Trainer Effectiveness* (Gower). His work has taken him all over the world and has involved directors of companies as well as managers and trainers.

Roger Bennett has worked in engineering, several business schools (including the International Management Centre, where he launched the UK's first masters degree in T&D) and has been a board director of two companies. He is the editor of the *Journal of European Industrial Training* and was series editor of the ITD's *Get In There* workbook and video package for the managers of training departments. He now runs his own business called The Management Development Consultancy.

About this book

What sort of book is this?

This book is designed to be a general resource, containing a wide range of practical ideas for running better workshops. We believe you will find the contents not only useful, but interesting. Our aim in writing it is to share ideas we have gained or developed from our collective experience, both of facilitating workshops and attending them.

The workshop format is increasingly used in training, education and development. If it were possible to find relevant statistics, it is certain that they would show rapid growth in the use of workshops in training and education alike over the last decade. There is no sign of any slowing in the rate of growth of these practical forms of training and development.

If you are new to facilitating workshops, we offer a range of suggestions, with enough detail for you confidently to try them out for yourself. For those of you with lots of experience of facilitating workshops, we believe you will be able to use or adapt ideas in this book to widen your own repertoire of successful workshop techniques.

Who is our book intended for?

We have three main groups of professional people in mind:

- Professional trainers and staff development specialists
- Managers who deal with training and staff development as part of their professional work
- Staff in higher and further education who increasingly use workshop formats as teaching/learning processes

That said, the best judge of whether this book will be of use to you is yourself. We invite you to flick through the contents to decide how the ideas in this book may be useful to you personally.

What is special about this book?

This book collects together a wide range of ideas and processes to select from, as you go about your task of running effective workshops. We chose not to include much discussion of the theory underlying the various techniques and methods we have described. Rather, we have offered them as a series of ideas that are worth trying. We have written the hundred items in the book in a way that each can be read—and used— on its own. This means that you do not have to start at the beginning and read through to the end. You can start and end anywhere that suits you.

Ten ways to use this book!

Dip in   This is a book that is meant to be dipped into, rather than read from cover to cover. It is full of things to do—it is a book to do rather than one to read. Scan the book for ideas you can use in your next workshop, and try them out.

Turn the ideas in the book into your own   We hope that you will use the book as a starting point and source of inspiration for your own ideas. Don't feel that you have to follow our suggestions to the letter— try them out in your own way. Find out how they work best for you.

Add to the pages   We have left plenty of white space for you to make your own notes and comments.

Review and reflect   Don't just use the book before your workshops; use it afterwards to help you to review your workshop and to reflect on how it went.

Make your own index   Get a pad of 'Post-it' notes and stick them to the margins of pages relating to items that you are using at a particular workshop. Place them so they stick out from the side of the book, serving as a quick index to the items you are using. You can write extra words or comments on the Post-its, to remind you of the ways you are going to adapt the items.

Share the book with participants at your workshops   Our experience is that an increasing number of people who attend our workshops are responsible for running their own workshops back in their own organizations. We have used many of the ideas in this book in such workshops.

Add your own ideas—and accidents!   We have left some blank pages at the end of the book for you to add your own ideas—including the 'accidents' that worked out well. Add also notes about the things you tried that didn't work out so well. We have learned at least as much from our mistakes as from our triumphs! Here are a couple of relevant quotations we like:

'If you haven't made any mistakes lately, you must be doing something wrong'.

'Mistake (n): strategy for learning something by not doing it right first time'.

Rearrange the book   If you would prefer to order the items in this book in a different way, tear up the book, or guillotine it, and re-organize the items to suit your purposes in a loose-leaf binder. (We have included a suggestion about tearing books up as a workshop technique—you may wish to use this book for such a purpose.)

Give out copies   You can use the whole book as a 'handout' if you are running a workshop on designing workshops. We used up most of our stock of pilot-editions of this book giving them to participants at our workshops.

Let us know how you get on   Write to any of us (care of the publishers) about ideas that work for you and which we have not included. We will be delighted to add your ideas (with due acknowledgement, of course) to the next edition of this book. Similarly, if you would like to share with us things that went hopelessly wrong for you, we shall be pleased to include them in the next edition (with due anonymity if you wish).

About the authors

Tom Bourner is Principal Lecturer at the University of Brighton in the Centre for Management Development. Originally trained as an economist, his current interests centre around more effective methods of management development. He is particularly interested in discovering new forms of action-based learning. He has written books on part-time students and workshop activities for induction programmes.

Vivien Martin is also at the University of Brighton in the Centre for Management Development where she works with an action learning programme in business research and manages the new Management Charter Initiative. She has wide experience in adult education and training, particularly in running workshops for developing managerial competence.

Phil Race is Professor of Educational Development at the University of Glamorgan. He conducts workshops throughout Britain for educational and commercial organizations on many topics, including open learning materials and developing competence. Phil has written widely on staff development, open learning and study skills.

1 What is a workshop?

A workshop is not a lecture—though it may contain some short episodes in lecture mode. A workshop is not a seminar. It is not just a discussion. If participants are clear about the nature and purposes of your workshops, they will get more out of them—and so will you.

Some definitions of a 'workshop'

The following definitions of a 'workshop' were given by participants at a workshop about workshop design:

- A group event at which all participants emerge able to do things better than they could at the beginning.
- An event at which each participant actively contributes for most of the time.
- An event at which participants learn a lot from each other.
- A training session at which the outcomes are dependent on the contributions of the participants rather than from input from the leader.
- A learning occasion based on the experience of the participants, rather than on the knowledge of the leader.
- A place where you get replacement parts fitted to your car at a price which surprises you and in a timescale that exceeds your expectations!

If you ask your participants to define a workshop, you'll get a range of answers—including amusing ones. More importantly, however, you will get a flavour of the kind of event they expect.

Variety is the spice of workshops

Most workshops last anything between a half-day to a week. It is even possible to have mini-workshops lasting as little as an hour. So what makes workshops different from lectures, courses, seminars or conferences? The variety. Any good workshop is based on a mixture of processes—most of which involve participants doing things rather than hearing about them. It could be said that workshops are based on experiential learning—particularly that which occurs in groups rather than alone. In this book we have collected suggestions for activity-based things you can try in your workshops, to provide plenty of choices and enable you to create variety and interest.

2 Workshop design for experiential learning

What is experiential learning?

It is convenient to think of knowledge, skills and attitudes as the three main fields in which learning can occur. Experiential learning is most useful when learning is sought in the areas of skills and attitudes.

The basis of experiential learning is that the learner is directly involved in an event and then draws conclusions from it. These 'conclusions' are the lessons. Experiential learning contrasts with learning based on the experience of others, which is what characterizes most conventional forms of learning from lectures, books etc. Experiential learning is essentially active rather than passive.

A model of experiential learning has been developed by David Kolb (1984) and offers a way of conceptualizing the process. He suggests a cycle of activities in experiential learning made up of four elements. These include concrete experience followed by observation/reflection, leading to the formation of abstract concepts and generalizations and finally the testing of the implications of concepts in new situations. This provides the starting point for the next loop in the cycle.

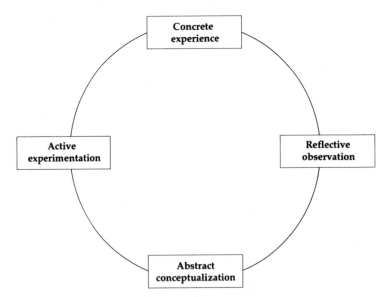

Figure 2.1 *Experiential learning cycle*

Stages in the cycle

Stage 1 *Concrete experience*
Personal involvement in experience.

Stage 2 *Reflective observation*
This stage involves forming a coherent picture of the experience by developing an answer to the question: 'What happened?' This is the first stage in understanding the experience and making sense of it.

Stage 3 *Abstract conceptualization*
At this stage the conceptualized experience is integrated with the rest of the personal construct system to discover any general implications.

Stage 4 *Active experimentation*
Testing the implications of the generalizations and practical application of the principles.

This has considerable significance in the design of workshops that are intended to affect competence or attitudes. It suggests a general format:

experience ⇒ reflection ⇒ conceptualization ⇒ experimentation

It is valuable to remember that all four stages should be included in an experiential workshop. And it is useful to remember that this is the sequence that will have most impact on learning.

This model also has considerable significance for the design of individual workshop activities and processes. This is the reason, for example, that simply watching an expert conducting an interview is unlikely to improve the observer's interviewing skills. It is the reason that the plenary/ debrief is so important as the final stage of an experiential exercise.

The model suggests that after an experiential activity the participants should be encouraged to consider the questions:

- 'What happened?' (reflection)
- 'What is the significance of what happened?' (conceptualization)
- 'What will I do as a result?' (experimentation)

3 The blurb

The 'blurb' is the technical term for a leaflet used to publicize a workshop. Most workshops use 'blurbs'. It is sometimes also known as a 'flyer'. You will have noticed how expert publishers are at designing book covers to attract readers. The same principles apply to advance publicity for workshops. This is particularly true when your workshop is one of several on offer (e.g. a parallel session at a conference). Yet so many examples of advance publicity are dull, monotonous and off-putting. This item is about ways of avoiding this.

Promoting your workshop

What do intending participants want to know?

- What is it about? (title and abstract)
- What exactly will I get out of it? (the objectives)
- How will it run? (outline programme)
- Who is giving it? (biographical details)

Your own aims regarding the blurb may include:

- Attracting potential participants to the general idea of the workshop
- Letting participants see exactly what the workshop may do for them
- Enabling participants to see how the workshop will unfold
- Giving participants an idea of what a nice workshop facilitator you are

The title

Here are some titles. Which workshop would YOU go to? (Don't worry about the topics—feel the titles!)

1 Performance Indicators for the Appraisal of Quality in the Design of Training Evaluation
2 Competence—Competitive or Collaborative?
3 An Introduction to the Basics of Writing Open Learning Materials
4 Computing for the Terrified!
5 Exploring Evaluation
6 Training Lecturers to Stop Teaching!

Here are our thoughts on those as titles.

1 Far too long. What on earth is the workshop really about? Looks heavy!
2 Nice one—got a bit of a ring to it.
3 Not good. I don't want to admit to being so 'low' that I need an introduction to the basics!

4 Much better. This is a nicer way of explaining that the workshop is suitable for beginners.

5 A good one—short and sharp. Also the word 'exploring' sounds attractive—it sounds participative rather than didactic.

6 This one hit a nail on the head—and still attracted large numbers of participants (all hoping the title did not really mean what it said!).

It is best if titles are short and sharp. If they can be made 'punchy' or vaguely amusing, so much the better.

Title and sub-title This is often a good way of having a punchy title—but giving a bit more detail without making the title itself longer. Here are some we thought up!

LEARNING STYLES
—myth or reality?

PERFORMANCE INDICATORS
—uses and abuses

DEFINING QUALITY IN EDUCATION
—never mind the teaching, feel the learning

The abstract For a start, it will not usually be called 'abstract'. It is the bit that explains why it is worth participating in the workshop. It may explain the importance of the topic. It may highlight the particular difficulties that the workshop will address. When you write this part of the blurb, try to sell your ideas to likely participants. Don't overdo it though—one good paragraph should suffice—not three pages!

The objectives What are people going to get out of your workshop? This is the time to be specific (and optimistic). Here are some 'do's' and 'don'ts' we have learned by trial and error!

Do . . .
• Make the objectives belong to the participant (e.g. 'by the end of the workshop you'll be able to . . . ' rather than 'at the end of the workshop participants will be able to . . . ')
• Start each objective with 'sharp' active words such as 'handle . . . ' 'use . . . ' 'discuss why . . . ' 'explain how to . . . '
• Keep it down to six or less objectives (long lists lose likely learners!)

Don't . . .
• Use words like 'understand' in the objectives—make the objectives clearer by using words that illustrate what participants will actually be able to do when they 'understand' the topic
• Make the objectives look too much like hard work—even when they are hard work. Take the sting out—make it seem reasonably likely that the person reading them will actually achieve them all
• Make any of the objectives look facile (we have seen objectives as patronizing as 'By the end of this workshop you'll be able to state that two-plus-two equals four')

Outline programmes   Since intending participants wish to weigh up whether the workshop will run in an interesting way, the outline programme needs to look interesting. Of course it needs to contain 'start' and 'stop' times, and 'coffee' and 'lunch' and so on. But it also needs to say a few words more than just content.

0930	Registration, coffee, informal introductions
0950	Introductory exercise (in pairs)
1030	Plenary brainstorm on modularism
1050	Syndicate task on prioritizing policy aims for modularism
1120	Coffee
1139	Syndicates report back
	and so on

Who is running the workshop?   Biographical details can be so boring! Phrases such as 'author of the best-selling text on modularism' tend to be redundant. If the text is a best-seller everyone should know about it anyway. If the bio-notes look warm and interesting, people may just think that the presenter is warm and interesting—and that is a first step in getting them to come to the workshop.

One of the authors of this book has been known to regularly use bio-notes along the following lines:

Phil Race was originally trained as a scientist, and eventually got doctored. However, he recovered from this and got interested in teaching and learning. For years he helped students learn chemistry—then he found that if he could do this he could help them learn anything, so he forgot about chemistry and concentrated on helping them learn anything. He did a lot of writing, so for a while they called him a 'Reader' at the college he lives in. When they found out he can't read, they gave him a Chair.

4 The blurb: a checklist

What should be included?

It can be a disaster if you omit something crucial such as the date of the workshop. What should you include in the blurb for your workshop? It really all depends on the workshop, so it is difficult to be too prescriptive. However, here is a checklist of items that you might consider including:

When
- date(s)
- duration
- times

Where
- venue
- map of location
- accommodation facilities

Why
- rationale for the workshop
- aims
- objectives

What
- title
- workshop structure
- content or themes
- outline programme

How
- your workshop approach (interactive and participative?)
- an indication of the specific processes (role plays, case studies, groupwork?)

Who
- details of the organizers/sponsors
- details of the presenters/facilitators
- an indication of the sort of participants that the workshop is designed for
- maximum number of participants

Cost
- workshop fee
- what the workshop fee does and does not include (workshop documents? lunch? refreshments? accommodation?)
- details of whom to write the cheque out to
- facilities to accept credit cards
- whether invoices will be issued
- discounts for participants paying for themselves (as opposed to being paid for by their organizations)
- discounts for participants from educational institutions
- discounts for the unwaged

APPLICATION FORM
- name
- title (i.e. Miss, Ms, Mrs, Mr, Dr, Prof, Sir)
- organization
- position in organization
- home address
- work address
- home telephone number
- work telephone number
- preferred name to be used at the workshop
- fax number (if there is one)

Closing date
- last date for applications
- last date for cancellations
- last date to get your money back if you cannot come

Address for further details
- also telephone number
- also fax number

Miscellaneous
- suggestion to any recipient who is not interested to pass the blurb on to someone else who might be
- suggestion that the recipient photocopy the blurb for any other people who they think might be interested in the workshop
- titles of other related workshops or short courses that you wish to promote
- covering letter

Warning: The more information that you include, the less impact any of it is likely to have. Also, if you can keep the blurb down to one sheet of A4 paper then you increase the likelihood that recipients of the blurb will photocopy it to other people whom they think might be interested.

5 Set a pre-workshop task

We do not intend that all participants should be asked to read Bloggs' key text on the subject before coming to the workshop. Only a few will do so, and tensions will be established between those who did and those who didn't. The more paperwork you supply in advance, the wider the knowledge gap between participants—so keep it simple.

Objectives
- To give participants the opportunity to do some useful preparation for the workshop.
- To bring participants closer to a common starting-point.
- To allow you to find out more about what participants already know.

The sort of pre-workshop task we have in mind usually involves no more than two sides of A4, to be returned to you, say, a week before the date of the workshop. If working at a distance, supplying a stamped addressed envelope works wonders in inducing people to undertake the task.

Purposes of the task

It is best if the task is structured into a number of definite steps, and the paper is clearly laid out with space for participants to address the questions you devise. Here are some suggestions for the purposes a pre-workshop task should aim to fulfil:

- To help you find out in advance how much participants already know about the topic (allowing you to judge where to start).
- To give you details of previous training that participants have experienced, and whether the group is going to be uniform or diverse.
- To allow you to meet in advance any strong views or opinions particular participants may hold. This gives you the opportunity to prepare to address such views at your workshop.
- To give participants a feeling of having shared something even before the workshop—e.g. if they chat informally before it begins, they may discuss some of the questions you asked in the exercise.
- To give participants the impression that you are trying conscientiously to find out exactly how best to make the workshop a success for them.
- To include open-ended questions such as 'which two issues do you think it will be most important to address at the workshop?' This allows you to prepare in advance for some of what may have been unanticipated.

- To open channels of communication between you and individual participants. The occasional participant will send you much more information than you asked for—it is often useful to know which participants these are in advance.

It is useful sometimes to build a couple of multiple-choice questions into the pre-workshop exercise. Often, multiple-choice questions are less threatening than open-ended ones—if participants really have no idea at this stage which option is correct, they are more willing to speculate by picking an option than they are willing to demonstrate their ignorance by writing a maybe-silly answer. At the workshop you can show how well you have done your homework by reporting that 'eight of you picked option A for question 5, no-one picked option B, but three of you picked each of options C and D; let's discuss the relative merits of these options now . . . '

Often it is possible to build into a pre-workshop exercise a question by which you can analyse the responses during the workshop. For example, you can type out all the replies (anonymously) to Question 3 and copy them onto an overhead transparency, and display participants' own words on the screen as a basis for exploration of the issue concerned. This helps to give participants a feeling of ownership of what is going on, and helps win their trust.

Rules for the task

Here are some rules to break as you see fit!

- Send the work to all participants.
- Send the same work to all participants unless you are asking different people to do different things.
- If you know that participants have different experience you could ask them to do different things to make best use of their expertise.
- Ask different participants to do different things so that they can each make a different presentation in the workshop.
- Ask participants who are able to get together to prepare work in pairs or groups before the workshop.
- If you ask people to prepare something, do use it in the workshop or they will be rather cross.
- Don't expect everyone to have done the work.
- Expect some to have misunderstood, misread or done it wrongly.
- Whatever you send out before the workshop will raise expectations of the workshop—be aware of the expectations you are encouraging.

Examples

Here are some examples of things we have asked participants to do before workshops:

- To read articles, papers and books
- To write short pieces sometimes with particular content or format
- To collect things
- To observe things
- To think about things

- To prepare talks or demonstrations or interviews
- To try things and report on what happened
- To make contact with others to prepare something
- To write out notes on 'where they're at' regarding the workshop topic
- To jot down what they want specifically from the workshop
- To make a preliminary action plan about what they intend to do after the workshop
- To make a list of questions they would like addressed during the workshop
- To prepare a 'T-chart' listing the advantages and disadvantages of a given procedure (see also below)
- To make an agenda for one of the sessions of the workshop

T-charts Asking people to make lists of opposites (or complementary things) is a useful way to start them thinking about important issues before a workshop. Simply asking them to prepare (and bring with them to the start of the workshop) a T-chart on suitable issues, means that all participants can have done some thinking about what they want to get out of the workshop. Suggest that they prepare lists of, say, five points under each of the two headings you suggest for their T-charts, and if possible bring their chart already on a flipchart sheet, so it can be displayed and discussed without wasting time transcribing it. A few ideas for the two 'sides' of T-charts are given below.

• Hopes: what I want from the workshop	• Fears: what I want to avoid at the workshop
• Things I already know about so-and-so	• Questions I have about so-and-so
• Benefits I see of developing so-and-so	• Risks associated with developing so-and-so
• Advantages of so-and-so	• Disadvantages of so-and-so
• Five reasons for . . .	• Five reasons against . . .
• Five ways of maybe doing it . . .	• Five ways likely to go wrong . . .
• Reasons why I think I can do it . . .	• Reasons why I think I can't do it . . .
• My ideas of the first few steps	• My ideas of the final stages

6 Joining instructions to participants

'Well done—you've passed the initiative test!' How often these are the first words to greet participants who have actually managed to make it to the workshop venue! This state of affairs can get a workshop off to a poor start—and a fragmented one—as participants arrive, hot and bothered, complaining about the inadequacy of joining instructions. All this is avoidable.

Getting them there

When a workshop is being held at the normal workplace of participants, there should be little or no need for detailed joining instructions. However, when workshops are attracting participants who are new to the venue, there are several points you should think about when writing joining instructions. Below, we have presented a checklist which can help to make it as straightforward as possible for participants to find the workshop venue.

Supply a good map   If participants may be coming by car, rail, taxi or on foot, the map needs to have clear directions from the railway station, from the nearest major road, and a sensible route for anyone coming on foot. Don't just use the map that has always been used—travel the last part of the route yourself (or get someone to check out the directions for you). It is often better to say 'turn left at the Elephant and Trunk' than to say 'turn left into Fothergill Street' as the streets marked on maps never seem to have nameplates on them!

Include directions to the workshop room   Phrases such as 'go to the third floor, and turn right at the top of the stairs' can be much more helpful than merely saying 'Room W309'.

Signpost the route from the main entrance anyway   This can be done quite quickly by sticking Post-its or pieces of coloured card or paper on doors and walls. Each sign needs an appropriate 'arrow' and a recognizable symbol of the workshop—the keyword from the title perhaps—and the date.

Be prepared early   There is always someone who arrives about an hour early—before you have put up the signs! Make sure that there is someone in the building looking out for participants like this—and offering them guidance regarding where they can wait in comfort.

Start with coffee   '0915–0945: Registration, coffee, informal introductions' should mean that everyone will be ready to start promptly at 0945.

What to bring with them?   Advice about the things participants need to bring with them is particularly important at residential workshops. When using hotels, most basics are usually provided, but in some conference centres life can be rather spartan for participants who didn't expect they needed to bring a towel, some soap, a radio perhaps, and so on. In such cases it is useful to provide a description of the sort of accommodation that will be available—conference centres can usually supply you with such a list to mail out to participants.

Similarly, make a list of papers and resources that participants may need during the workshop.

7 Your facilitator's toolkit

Normally you can expect to arrange in advance with the people in charge of the workshop venue such things as overhead projectors, flipcharts, room layout, syndicate rooms, and provision of refreshments. However, it is safest to have your own personal toolkit of smaller items—some obvious—and some not so obvious!

Things you may need

We have not attempted to put these suggested items in order of priority as the prime need is the need of the moment at any given time. We suggest that you check out which of them you need in your kit—and add additional ones that particularly apply to the sort of workshops you run.

Overhead projector (OHP) pens   If you want individuals or syndicates to write the products of workshop tasks on acetate sheets, have at least as many pens as participants—preferably double the number (pens, like facilitators, dry up!).

Plenty of acetate sheets   For workshop tasks, you don't need the heavy duty acetate that is designed for photocopying—simple 'write-on film' is cheaper. Even when the venue claims to supply acetate sheets, it usually supplies only four!

Scissors   If you want to give out small pieces of acetate (e.g. a quarter of an A4 sheet) to participants, don't rely on being able to tear the acetate. Some acetate is impossible to tear.

Flipchart pens   Even the best-equipped workshop venues tend only to provide about four of these. If you want your participants to split into syndicates, and produce flipcharts for their report-back, it is useful if each syndicate can have at least two different-coloured flipchart pens.

Blu-tack   This is essential if you are going to fix flipchart sheets to walls, and it is surprising how much you can get through at a productive workshop.

Two or three Post-it pads   You will find in this book a number of suggested uses of Post-its. You will probably think of many more uses for these portable, highly versatile visual aids. Unlike flipcharts, Post-its can be regrouped, clustered, and manipulated in all sorts of ways. Post-its stuck to flipcharts offer the workshop equivalent of word-processing flexibility.

A small screwdriver It helps if you can change the fuse in a plug yourself without having to wait for an electrician. (Carry a fuse too—it doesn't take up much room.) Also, quite often some tightening-up or adjustment may be needed to get the best out of the overhead projector.

A six-inch (15 cm) plastic ruler Apart from the obvious uses of this device, it can be stuck adjacent to the top edge of an A4 sheet of blank paper to make a 'mask' to cover up parts of overhead transparencies. This allows you to reveal the contents a little at a time, without the sheet dropping off and revealing your all as the sheet gets towards the bottom of its travel!

A few ordinary pens and pencils Unbelievable as it may seem, Mr K A Jones will arrive at your workshop without any means whatsoever of writing. Giving him a pen will not only make him a cooperative participant, but also a friend for life.

A glue-stick Quite often, it is useful to be able to stick overhead transparencies onto a flipchart, so that their contents remain available to anyone who wishes to go back to them later. This particularly applies to overheads produced by syndicates at your workshop. Having overheads up on the wall as well as flipcharts adds to the feeling of participant ownership that makes for a healthy workshop.

Some meths and tissues! One of the authors of this book attracts a lot of comments about the miniature 'Glenfiddich' bottle in his travel bag—especially when he declares that it contains meths! This common solvent has a variety of uses at workshops, including cleaning the glass lenses and mirrors of overhead projectors (which are often unbelievably grimy!) and 'editing' overheads written with permanent pens.

A hedgehog (One of those rubber things you put on your finger to make it easier to separate sheets of paper from a pile.) This can help speed up the task of giving everyone a copy of a handout. A good substitute in an emergency is a rubber band round a strategic finger.

A translucent LCD clock Yes, they do exist. When you particularly want to alert participants to the time (e.g. during a five-minute brainstorm) you can place such a device on the overhead projector, and the time will be projected onto the screen 'live' for all to see. (The fixed clock on the wall is normally displaying the time in Bangladesh—and only correct exactly twice each day.)

A kitchen (or photographic) timer Sometimes you will want to keep participants to time 'audibly'—e.g. when giving each syndicate in turn four minutes to report its findings. (Nothing annoys more people quickly than that report-back which goes on, and on, and on.) Something that 'bleeps' or 'buzzes' is rather kinder than having to take chairperson's action and ask people to shut up!

A very small torch One of those 'pen-shaped' torches is ideal. Besides the uses arising at the workshop (e.g. when Gladys drops one of her contact lenses), such a torch is reassuring when your train has a lighting failure on becoming delayed by a broken rail in the middle of the Severn Tunnel.

Some kitchen roll   This can be handy to mop up spilled coffee or wine (if you're lucky), and to sort out disasters such as leaking flipchart pens.

Some rubber bands   These are useful to roll up flipcharts you want to keep (maybe to transcribe for 'workshop products').

Some 'Tipp-ex'   This is very useful for 'whiting-out' mistakes on flipcharts, as well as for editing materials you may want to photocopy.

Some masking tape   This can be used to fix all sorts of things to all sorts of other things—and in emergencies can even be used to repair the plumbing in foreign hotels!

Some paper-clips   Useful for preparing 'wads' of handout materials ready to issue to participants, and for keeping your own papers and overheads in 'clumps' rather than chaos.

Something to keep your bits and bobs in   If you have got to scrabble around collecting your kit before each workshop you run, sooner or later you will forget something important—or miss your train. Having just one 'thing' to grab saves a lot of mental energy. An ideal invention is the sort of soft bag with a zip used for toiletries. This is flexible enough to be stuffed into briefcase or travel bag, and big enough not to get lost under your handouts. When running residential workshops, however, take care that your real toilet bag doesn't end up in the work-shop room, with your 'bits and bobs' bag on your dressing table!

Some coins   Besides being of immediate use in the vicinity of coffee machines, these can be used to pin down those occasional overhead transparencies that seem to wish to curl into a ball under the heat of the projector.

A5 sheets of card—or plain file cards   These have all sorts of uses. They can be stuck to room doors to identify syndicate areas. They can be folded once so that they can stand on desks or tables as participants' names cards. In informal groups without tables they can be used as 'foot-cards' so that every participant can clearly see each name in the group.

Asking people to put their own names on the cards (using bold flipchart pens) ensures that all the names are spelled absolutely cor-rectly (there is no quicker way to alienate a participant than to spell her name wrongly). Also, participants have a good idea about exactly what name they prefer to be called by at your workshop. Dr Patricia Boyd-Hamilton may well prefer to be called 'Pat'.

A holepunch   Sometimes you may be using ring-binders to issue workshop documentation. It can be very much appreciated if you have a holepunch available, so that participants can add additional handouts and notes to their collected papers. Remember to take the right sort of holepunch!

And for advanced facilitators!

The British Rail full passenger timetable   Expertise in interpreting this may endear you to many a participant who has travelled a long way to be at your workshop!

Your jump leads   Producing a favourable review of the workshop as a whole from K A Jones, who chooses to illuminate the car park all day with his headlights!

8 Introducing the facilitators

First impressions

There is no second chance to make a good first impression. The first few minutes of a workshop can be 'make or break' minutes.

There is a notion that when one person meets another they allow the other person a certain number of 'credibility' points. These are things that indicate how much the newly met person conforms to expectations, perhaps in terms of their role in a particular situation, perhaps of their knowledge or skills. This has implications for workshop facilitators if they are working with people who do not know them, as it is possible to lose all your 'credibility' points in one go, just by dressing in what the participants think to be an inappropriate way, making an inappropriate remark, or not introducing yourself in the way they expect. It is tempting to want to shock a little; workshops are often about changing attitudes, but this is not likely to be achieved if trust is lost.

However, if you want to introduce yourself a little differently, here are some methods:

- Invite participants to ask you anything they would like to know and perhaps decline to answer some questions.
- Put up an overhead projector (OHP) slide detailing main points of information about yourself.
- Give out a CV.

It is human nature to make assumptions about people based on first impressions—your participants will be busily making all sorts of assumptions about you from the moment they see you—or from the moment they read information about you in the workshop documentation.

9 Interviewing the facilitator

Objectives
- To enable the participants to find out more about yourself as facilitator
- To model the process of self-disclosure

People usually form first impressions within a few minutes of meeting someone new. So it pays to get off on the right foot. If you want to introduce yourself a little differently, you may like to try this idea.

Before the workshop, explain the idea of 'facilitator interviews' to the host or sponsor of the workshop. Point out that it means that they won't have to memorize an introduction for you. Point out also that it will give you an opportunity to model behaviour that you want to encourage in the participants: self-disclosure as a way of sharing experience.

At the start of the workshop the host or sponsor explains to the participants that this will be a novel form of introducing the facilitator. The facilitator will be 'interviewed' by a participant. Ask for a volunteer (or select a participant) to be the interviewer. Provide a sheet with the following questions listed on them:

1 What is your name?
2 Where do you come from?
3 What do you hope to be doing in career terms in five years' time?
4 What are you feeling right now?
5
6
7 What is one expectation that you have for the workshop?

Explain that the 'interview schedule' contains some basic questions and some missing ones. Ask the interviewer to think of a couple of questions to fill the gaps but not to tell you what they will be. If the interviewer seems to be encountering any difficulty then invite other participants to suggest questions.

Comments
Invite the interviewer to ask supplementary questions during the interview.

Variations
There are various ways of modifying this activity. The questions can be varied. The number of questions can be varied. The balance between 'pre-planned' and 'spontaneous' questions can be changed. The host/sponsor can be the interviewer.

10 Introducing participants

The following procedures are to help the participants to begin to get to know one another, and to develop confidence in the group. (Some of the procedures below can take quite some time, and are therefore unsuitable for short workshops.)

Procedures

Introducing course participants who are new to each other
- You can ask everyone to say what name they would like to be called by and a little about their work or why they are at the workshop.
- If the group is large or the participants likely to be nervous, it may be unkind to ask everyone to say something right at the beginning. Another way to get them talking right away is to pair them and ask them to introduce themselves to the other and to tell each other something about themselves. You can then ask each to introduce the other to the whole group, or you could widen the process by pairing the pairs several times.

Mutual interviewing
- Brainstorm with the group 'things that you'd like to know about each other in the context of this group'. Identify and flipchart main themes that emerge from the brainstormed material.
- The participants form pairs and one person interviews another to gather this information (and anything else that the two think of and wish to share). Five minutes is probably about the right time for this part of the activity.
- Those who have interviewed stay where they are while the others move round and interview someone that they have not previously met.
- Everyone prepares for a couple of minutes (organizes their notes, etc.) to introduce the person they interviewed.
- In turn, individuals address the group, introducing the person that they have interviewed. About two minutes each is the right amount of time.

Since this activity involves each person addressing the whole group, it is clearly most suitable for workshops with relatively small numbers of participants (up to about 12).

Introducing participants who already know some of the others
- Ask everyone to pair with someone they do not know at all, or who they know only slightly. Then ask them to introduce themselves and find out something about the other. Each then introduces the other to the whole group or to another pair until everyone has been introduced.
- If participants are used to speaking in groups, they could each be asked to give a three-minute presentation of themselves and why they are in the workshop.

11 Paired introductions

Objectives
- To enable participants to introduce themselves within the workshop
- To enable participants to meet—and feel more comfortable with—some of the others in the workshop whom they don't already know
- To form small groups for subsequent activities

Invite the participants to look round the room and identify the other people they don't (yet) know. Explain the process as follows:

Ask each participant to find a partner from among those whom they don't know. Each pair to spend eight minutes introducing themselves to each other (four minutes each way). Then ask each pair to find another pair and in that foursome each person to spend two minutes introducing his or her partner to the other pair (eight minutes in total). Suggest that the participants don't make notes during this process but rely on their listening skills.

It is helpful if you act as timekeeper for this activity: e.g. you could announce the end of four minutes, eight minutes, 12 minutes and 16 minutes.

Variations
One variation is that you need not discourage participants making notes. The activity will then be less stressful but also less effective in developing supportive relationships.

If the number of participants is small, then instead of forming four-somes you could ask each person to introduce his or her partner to the rest of the group.

Another variation is that you can set the agenda for the introductions. For example, you could flipchart some of the following questions:

What is your name?
Where are you from?
What do you do for a living?
If you didn't do that what would you like to do?
What else have you done?
What would you like to be doing in career terms in five years' time?
How are you feeling right now?
What do you want to get out of this workshop?

If you include the last question you could follow this up with a round in which each person introduces his or her partner by name and explains what he or she wants to get out of the workshop. At this stage you could flipchart the 'wants' as input into the workshop process.

12 Be kind to yourself

If you don't take care of yourself you won't be much good to others . . .
At the risk of being patronizing, we suggest:

Look after yourself   In terms of general health—be aware of your
weight, smoking, drinking, etc., and do something about it if it is not
healthy.

Enjoy yourself   Try to enjoy the free things in life; sunlight, trees,
clouds, views, smiles, ideas, sounds . . .

Respect yourself   Be protective of your own needs and wants; be
assertive enough to say no when appropriate. Don't let the workshop
participants make demands on you all the time (especially in
residentials).

Surprise yourself   Try changing your attitude towards problems, for
example. One of us coined the word 'probortunities' pointing out that
each problem contains an opportunity. The next time you think you
have got a problem, remember that it is an opportunity too!

Indulge yourself   Next time you feel stressed, take a break. Use your
imagination to get out of a situation you don't want to be in—visualize
a better future and make an action plan to get there!

Distance yourself   From things that you know stress you too much.
Accept that different situations suit different people and discover how
you work best. Seek out situations in which you flourish. Avoid triggers
which are negative for you; e.g. if confrontation is stressful for you,
avoid letting situations develop confrontationally, intervene at an early
stage and set up negotiations.

Pace yourself   Deal with one thing at a time. Sort out which are really
important and which are just clamouring for attention and noisy. Do
them in the order you think is important and tell some that they will
have to wait!

Next time you feel 'got at' take a few slow, deep breaths, preferably at
an open window (not one facing out onto a busy road and letting in
exhaust fumes), while deciding how best to look after yourself.

13 How to run a disastrous workshop

If you know how to make something worse, then you know how to make it better. A useful technique for problem solving is to look for ways to make a situation as bad as it can be, then to examine all these ways looking for how to reverse them. This should lead you to a recipe for brilliant success.

- Don't plan anything
- Don't book a venue
- Don't advertise the workshop
- Don't tell anyone about it
- Tell everyone the wrong time and venue
- Book an unsuitable venue:
  - too small
  - too large
  - too dark
  - stuffy
  - smelly
  - noisy
  - bad acoustics
  - cold/hot
  - no drinks
  - no food
  - unfriendly
  - no chairs/tables
  - no equipment
- Don't have coffee breaks—or any breaks
- Make sure that the only available refreshment is coffee
- Don't introduce yourself
- Don't give participants an opportunity to introduce themselves
- Talk all the time
- Don't let anyone else talk or do anything
- Don't tell anyone what the programme is
- Don't have a programme
- Don't tell anyone your aims
- Start late
- Go to lunch late
- Finish late

- Don't tell anyone you are the facilitator
- Tell everyone it is much too hard for them to do
- Keep repeating the same activity
- Don't bother to debrief any of the activities
- Don't make eye contact with anyone . . .
- Don't send out a map
- Set 15-minute coffee breaks . . . when the coffee is being served in another building
- Don't include the option of a vegetarian lunch
- Say 'I am the world's expert on . . .'

(You could add to this list . . .)

Then look at each point and *reverse* it, and this becomes your *checklist for running a good workshop*—plan everything, book a venue, advertise the workshop, etc. Save your checklist and add to it each time you plan a workshop.

14 Paying attention to the competition

Hierarchy of needs

According to psychologist Abraham Maslow we each have five types of need:

1 *Physiological needs*. These are the most basic needs required for physical survival and include air, food, water and so on.
2 *Safety needs*. These are needs for security and the absence of threat and fear. They are future orientated and include the need to ensure that the physiological needs will continue to be met in the near future.
3 *Affiliation needs*. These include the needs for acceptance, belonging, support, affection, friendship and love.
4 *Esteem needs*. These needs include self-esteem and the esteem of others. They include the need for personal feelings of achievement and to be perceived by others as competent. We each need self-respect and the respect of significant others. The latter is manifest in the need for such things as attention, recognition and status.
5 *Self-actualization needs*. These are the needs for personal growth: to move towards becoming what one is capable of being. They manifest themselves in a need to understand oneself and transcend one's limitations, to come closer to attaining one's human potential.

In addition to this classification of types of needs, Maslow offered the additional idea that these five types constitute a hierarchy of priorities. If you are hungry (physiological) then you will be less concerned about sharing a social identity or sense of social belonging with others (affiliation). You will be less worried about transcending your current limitations (self-actualization) if you are afraid of losing your job (safety).

According to Maslow, it is only after the physiological needs have been satisfied that the safety needs take priority. Only after these have been satisfied do the affiliation needs assume top priority. When these have been satisfied then esteem needs take priority. And when esteem needs have been satisfied, the need for self-actualization moves into prime position. In other words the different needs form a ladder of priorities.

Why is all this important when you are running a workshop? If your workshop is concerned with, say, developing interviewing skills, you can assume that your participants have at some level a 'need' to develop their interviewing skills (either that, or you must have produced some very strange pre-workshop publicity). However, if your workshop room is too hot then the attention of many of your participants will be captured by their physiological need to be cooler.

Physiological needs

Maslow's hierarchy of priorities suggests a range of factors to which you, as facilitator, should attend, to ensure that you retain the attention of your participants. Some of these, the ones that pertain to physiological needs, are likely to be particularly important at the start of the workshop. You can make sure that these are OK at the outset. Here is a checklist of basic physiological factors:

- Temperature. Is your room too hot or too cold? You may wish to check before you start the workshop that you are able to control the temperature of the room that you will be working in.
- Noise. Will the traffic outside the room prevent some people from hearing?
- Light. Is your room gloomy? Lights that are too bright can be a distraction as well as a room that is too dark. Are any of the lights likely to cause a distraction by flickering?
- Ventilation. Is the room stuffy? Can you open a window without introducing too much traffic noise? Is it worth opening all the windows during the breaks for an 'air change'?
- Thirst. Is there coffee, tea, fruit juice and/or water available? Are these available 'on tap' at any time? If not, are there enough breaks to ensure that participants don't get thirsty?
- Hunger. Do you want to have a plate of biscuits available?
- Comfort breaks. It is very difficult to concentrate if what you really want right now is to urinate. Plenty of comfort breaks is one solution. An explicit ground-rule that anyone can take a comfort break at any time without a 'by your leave' is another.

Attention to these factors at the start of the workshop will help the participants to feel nurtured and allow them to give all their attention to the job in hand. Then ask your senses to tell you if any of these factors need adjustment subsequently.

So far, we have concentrated on the physiological needs. If participants at the workshop are experiencing any unmet needs then some of their awareness will be unavailable to them for the purposes of the workshop. Maslow's needs classification suggests a range of questions for addressing this issue.

Safety needs

Asking the participants to be aware of the above factors (temperature, noise, lighting, ventilation, etc.) and to let you know if they feel that any require adjusting, will help the participants feel secure that due attention will be paid to these factors. Sorting out ground-rules at the outset also helps to create safety.

Affiliation needs These are especially important where few of the participants know each other at the outset. Paying particular attention to introductions helps here. Introductions take time and at a short workshop time is at a premium. In this situation, it is more important that the participants should get to know one or two of the other participants reasonably well than that there should be superficial introductions to everyone else at the workshop.

Esteem needs Introductions are valuable in this area too. The very opposite of getting esteem needs met is to feel like a non-person, and introductions allow participants to establish their identity at the workshop. Providing participants with the opportunity to tell the others briefly of their experience, knowledge or skills in the workshop topic is another useful idea for meeting esteem needs. Helping participants to feel respect for themselves and for their achievements is helpful too. So when you notice good work (including a high level of participation and energy) by individuals and by the group take the time to acknowledge it.

Self-actualization needs Since your workshop is probably about participants transcending limitations and moving closer towards their potential in some way or other, most of the rest of this book is concerned with these needs.

15 Participants' aims

When you were preparing your workshop you will have developed, no doubt, a set of aims to guide yourself. This is especially important if you are developing a workshop with another (or others). No doubt you will also have included these aims (or a summary of them) in your 'flyer' for the workshop or in whatever means you are using to publicize your workshop. And, no doubt, you will refer to these aims at the start of the workshop.

All of this is sensible and helps to establish a 'contract' between you and the participants, ensuring your respective expectations are in line. But these are *your* aims. Your participants will have their own ideas of what they want to experience at the workshop. Finding out the aims of the participants for the workshop is a way of valuing the participants, and obtaining useful information.

It can be useful to ask participants to express their aims using some (or all) of the following 'pointer' question-words: what? how? when? who? where? why?

For example, at a workshop for training writers of open learning materials, participants could be asked for their aims as follows:

- Why do you wish to write open learning materials?
- What topics will you choose for the materials you write?
- Who are you writing the materials for?
- Where do you anticipate these materials being used?
- When do you wish to have a working draft of the materials?
- How would you like this workshop to help you get started with your writing?

16 Workshop expectations

When you are running a workshop with a new group of participants (and particularly if the participants don't already know each other), it is useful to ask a quite open-ended question regarding their expectations of the workshop.

Displaying an overhead such as the one shown in Fig. 16.1, and giving participants small pieces (e.g. quarter-sheets) of acetate and an OHP pen, is a quick way of gathering participants' expectations.

Workshop expectations

Please write on a small piece of acetate a few words about what you personally most wish to gain from this workshop

Please write your name

Figure 16.1   *A sample overhead, asking for participants' views*

The acetate slips can then be shown in turn on the overhead projector, and individual participants can be invited to enlarge on particular expectations (and to say a few words of introduction about themselves if they wish).

It is also useful to give participants this chance to write their names—it helps you work out who is who—and sometimes at this stage you find that you have got someone not on your list (e.g. a substitute).

Using a glue-stick, the acetate slips can each be pasted lightly on to a flipchart, so that you can keep your participants' expectations in sight for the rest of the workshop. This allows you to refer now and then to specific expectations, enhancing the feeling of ownership that participants develop over the workshop content and processes.

17 A learning agreement

Establishing a learning agreement with the participants will make it more likely that all participants at the workshop are clear about their expectations. It helps to clarify the limits of the workshop. Also, it helps to clarify the role of the participants in getting their own learning objectives met.

1 Briefly explain the reason for having a learning agreement.
2 Ask participants to spend five minutes privately writing down answers to the following four questions:

'What do you want to achieve as a result of attending this workshop?'
'What would you have to do to ensure that you achieve it?'
'What might stop you achieving what you want from the workshop?'
'How will you know when you've achieved it?'

3 Ask the participants to form pairs and spend 10 minutes exchanging their answers to the first question above (the other three questions are more for their own consideration and form the basis of an agreement with themselves).
4 Reconvene and then ask each participant to introduce his/her partner by saying what they wish to get from the workshop. Flipchart the points that emerge and post the flipchart.

Establishing a learning contract

A learning agreement can be developed into a *learning contract*. This is a more formal strategy which can be the basis of a learning programme by defining exactly what the participant plans to do, and what support and accreditation the institution offers if the programme is based in an educational establishment.

The contract describes the learning plan the participant will follow, the targets set with review dates, and the assessment procedures and timing. The contract is signed by both parties, the participant and a representative of the institution who is usually the tutor or programme supervisor.

A learning contract usually provides for reflection on previous experience relevant to the current programme for which the participant might want to claim some credit. It focuses on the individual's current knowledge and skills and sets targets for new knowledge and skills. It should outline the steps the individual needs to take to reach the targets set and should indicate how this will be done and how it will be assessed.

The learning contract is likely to be a substantial document, taking some time to prepare. It is more appropriate for a long learning programme than for a short programme or workshop where a learning agreement is usually sufficient.

18 Making your own aims explicit

It is a good idea to be very explicit about your aims for the workshop. This will help you to design the workshop. It will help you to identify the themes to be covered and appropriate workshop processes. Clarifying your aims will also help you to write the 'blurb' or 'flyer' for the workshop. One thing that potential participants will expect to see on material publicizing the workshop is a statement of your aims for the workshop. They need this to decide if it will be worth while to them.

It has become conventional to make a distinction between aims expressed in a tutor-orientated way from those expressed in a participant-orientated way. Tutor-orientated aims state what the tutor wants to achieve. Participant-orientated aims state what the outcome should be for the participant.

The following set of aims could be regarded as tutor-orientated:

The aims of this workshop are:

- *To introduce the principles of self- and peer-assessment.*
- *To provide some experience of using self- and peer-assessment.*
- *To enable participants to consider the application of self- and peer-assessment in their own work.*

Examples of participant-orientated aims are as follows:

By the end of this workshop participants will be able to:

- *Discuss the principles of self- and peer-assessment.*
- *List significant lessons about self- and peer-assessment from their experience of it within the workshop.*
- *Begin to design the application of self- and peer-assessment in their own work.*

You might be sceptical about describing the latter formulation as participant-orientated. You might think that these aims are really still tutor-orientated but are just more specific and expressed in terms of the behaviour of the participants. And we might be inclined to agree with you. If you subscribe to the notion that as 'teachers' and 'trainers' all we can really do is to provide an environment and processes that participants can use for their own learning then you might want to reflect this in how you express your aims for the workshop.

For example:

Our aims in this workshop are to give you the opportunity to:

- *Share your experience of self- and peer assessment.*
- *Discuss the principles of self- and peer-assessment.*
- *Experience self- and peer-assessment, drawing significant lessons from it.*
- *Begin to design the application of self- and peer-assessment in your own work.*

This formulation makes it clear that these are the aims of the tutors/facilitators (the aims of the participants will be identified at the start of the workshop!). However, they are expressed in such a way that potential participants are forewarned that responsibility for learning will rest with the participants themselves.

19 Personal aims and contributions

Objectives
- To identify what the participants want from the workshop.
- To help participants become more aware themselves of what they want from the workshop.
- To find out what the participants are able and willing to contribute to the workshop.
- To help participants to take responsibility for the experience and outcomes of the workshop.

Give each participant a sheet of flipchart paper (A1 size). Ask them to write their name at the bottom of the sheet then draw a horizontal line across the centre and head the top half 'aims' and the bottom half 'contributions' as in Fig. 19.1. Place a large box of flipchart pens on the floor in the centre of the room. Then ask the participants to spend the next 10 minutes listing their own personal aims for the workshop and what they are able and willing to contribute to it. Ask them to write large and legibly with the flipchart pens as the results will be displayed round the room afterwards.

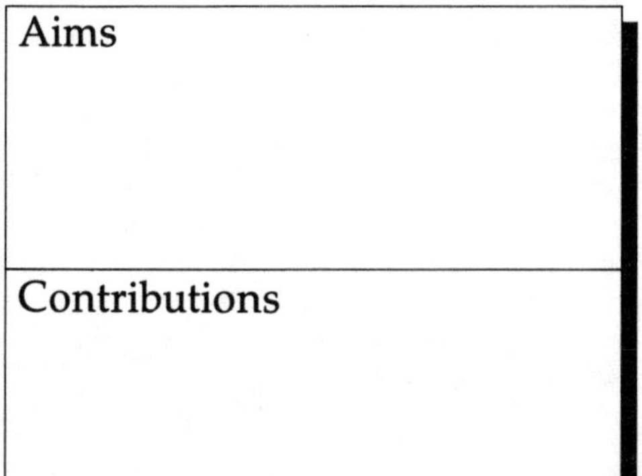

Aims

Contributions

Name

Figure 19.1   Flipchart for collecting aims and contributions

After 10 minutes give each participant a small wad of Blu-tack and ask them to fix their flipchart on the wall.

Allow about five minutes for the participants to mill around and read each other's flipcharts.

Ask participants to spend a few minutes considering the following questions:

- What can you do to achieve your aims for this workshop?
- How will you know when you have achieved your aim(s)?

20 Reworked aims

Objectives
- To demonstrate to the workshop participants that you are taking their personal aims seriously.
- To take their personal aims seriously.
- To process the information on aims provided by the participants.

We have suggested several ways of recording the personal aims of the participants. This activity is a way of using these aims to good effect in longer workshops (two or more days) where it can be useful to give participants the opportunity to reflect on their aims, and fine-tune them to the emerging circumstances of the workshop.

- At the end of the day, take the personal workshop aims that have been disclosed by the participants and classify them into broad themes. Choose a heading for each broad theme.
- Rewrite the aims on flipchart paper under the theme headings. When you do this you are bound to have a number of aims that you can't classify under your existing theme headings—the theme heading for these is 'miscellaneous'!
- The next morning, start by displaying the 'classified aims' and briefly discuss each theme and how it relates to the activities of the workshop.
- In the light of what you discover in working through the participants' aims for the workshop you are likely to want to make changes to your original programme.

In a series of workshops or a long residential it is helpful to review progress from time to time. The list of reworked aims can be the basis of each review and can be used visually by ticking or crossing off each aim as it has been achieved. This gives a satisfying sense of progress!

The discussions held at each review can help to re-focus on the outstanding aims, can help to explore the group's consciousness of the process of learning and can re-energize the group to progress further.

21 Prioritizing objectives

We have already mentioned the benefits of starting a workshop with a clear set of objectives—and adding to the list particular additional objectives that may arise from participants' expectations. It can be useful to perform some operations with the workshop objectives, to find out which objectives are most important to participants; to help participants to think more deeply about them; and to steer the emphasis of the workshop along the lines wished by participants.

The following steps provide a quick and effective way of establishing the relevance and relative importance of workshop objectives.

- Display the list of objectives on an overhead transparency or flipchart.
- Ask participants to give each objective a score out of a total of (say) 20 points (i.e. to divide up 20 points among the objectives), reflecting how important or useful each objective seems to promise to be. Explain that it is all right to give some objectives zero-rating—or even to allocate all 20 points to one objective that seems really important.
- Ask every participant to give you their points ratings for objective number one, writing the numbers up beside the objective. Repeat until you have a series of numbers alongside all the objectives.
- Tot up the total score for each objective—the most important ones will usually stand out clearly with highest scores.
- Discuss with participants any objectives that attracted very low scores—it may be worth dropping them (and associated activities) from the workshop programme (and substituting something elaborating on more popular objectives).

These procedures allow you to find out which objectives are of interest to most participants, and which are only of interest to some. This analysis could be put to useful purpose in the design of syndicate tasks (e.g. asking the three participants who gave high ratings to objective no. 3 to form a syndicate specially to address that objective, while other syndicates were working on something else).

Quite often, you will be surprised by the differences between participants' scorings. You can turn this into productive discussion, e.g. by inviting the person who gave 10 points to objective no. 5 to explain why it was felt to be so important, and asking someone who rated it zero to reply.

22 What participants know already

Objectives
- To identify where the workshop participants are starting from.
- To identify to the participants (including yourself as facilitator) what knowledge, skills and experience are available as resources to the workshop.

There are various ways of doing this. They include:

1 Asking the participants to say, when they introduce themselves, what their background in the topic is. Be careful here, as participants at the outset of a workshop are likely to understate their levels of expertise. Their natural modesty will prevail . . . and they are unlikely to want to carry the burden of the responsibility of being an expert. It is better to ask them for their experience than their level of expertise. Experience is more factual than expertise so they need not make judgements about their own competence. For example, consider a workshop on supervising postgraduate research students. In this case, the participants could be asked to say, when they introduce themselves, what experience they have had of research degree supervision—either as supervisor or supervisee.

2 A quiz. The danger with this approach is that this can be threatening to participants. Quizzes have all the connotations of tests. So, if you do this, wait until you done some work in establishing the safety of the workshop. Alternatively, you could have an anonymous quiz. The participants write answers on sheets that they don't sign. This is likely to produce humorous answers but it is likely to be more time-consuming.

3 Starting with a brainstorm using questions such as 'What ways can you think of to . . .' or 'What happens if . . .' or 'How many different types . . . can you think of'?

An attractive feature of these suggestions is that they engage the participants from the outset so they can 'double' as energy raisers. They are most useful when the object of the workshop is to help the participants acquire knowledge rather than develop skills or affect attitudes.

It is most unlikely that all the workshop participants will be starting from a similar level of expertise or knowledge. Usually, they will be starting from very different points. You may therefore wish to choose activities and processes that capitalize on this diversity. Typically the more active processes (various forms of groupwork) will do this whereas more passive forms of delivery (such as lectures) do not.

23 Questions for the facilitator

Objectives
- To give the participants an opportunity to find out more about the facilitator.
- To encourage participants to contribute from the start of the workshop.

When people arrive to register for a workshop, give them a copy of your biography, ask them to read it through before the workshop starts and to mark (e.g. underline) any parts of it that they find interesting or intriguing.

When the workshop participants are seated, explain that you would like them to think up questions that elaborate parts of the biography and give them a few minutes to do so.

Ask for volunteers to ask their questions. After each question ask if there are any more questions on that topic. This will encourage the less forthcoming to ask their questions and give more coherence to your responses.

This activity gives people 'something to do' when they arrive at a workshop. This is most useful when the participants are all new to each other—in that situation some people will find it difficult to introduce themselves to others.

This activity is mostly a device to introduce yourself so don't let it get out of hand and take up too much time (no matter how much you enjoy talking about yourself). Ten minutes maximum is about right.

24 Roles of a workshop facilitator

Participants' disappointment with a workshop is likely to occur when expectations are not met. Expectations are unlikely to be met when they differ between the facilitator and the participants or between the participants themselves. One area where expectations may differ is about the roles of the workshop facilitator.

Obtaining participants' views

Here is how to enable participants to air their views about the roles of the workshop facilitator, identify any differences that may exist and develop a mutual understanding. First, invite the participants to express the various roles, attitudes, and behaviours they expect of the facilitator. List these on a flipchart or OHP. Then share a previously prepared set of your intended roles. A sample set (for illustration) is shown below. You can then proceed to reconcile the two lists.

Example

Roles of a facilitator

1 Develops a programme of workshop activities
2 Helps to develop a climate that participants can use to learn
3 Shares ideas
4 Provides handouts
5 Serves as a model
6 Raises questions
7 Guides discussion
8 Restates ideas
9 Challenges thinking
10 Summarizes

Possible discussion questions

- What do you expect in a facilitator that I do not intend to provide?
- What is the source of your expectations? (prior educational experience? wishful thinking?)
- What do I intend to provide that you did not expect?
- Do you anticipate any problems reconciling your expectations with my planned role? If so, what can I or you do to prevent such problems?

Variations   This approach can be used for addressing participants' expectations about other aspects of a workshop. For example, questions could be:

How do you expect teaching/learning methods to differ between a workshop and a short course? What attitudes are likely to enable you to get most out of this workshop?

25 Workshop interviews

If you intend to use workshops frequently as part of a longer programme or course of study, you might consider running group interviews in workshop style rather than individual ones.

The agenda might range from plain 'Should this person be admitted to the course?' to *Is this the right course for this person?*

Some issues can be addressed by:

- Using the session to give an example of the way in which participants will work and learn.
- Allowing prospective participants to meet and talk about hopes and fears.
- Enabling more detailed and specific questioning about the course than individuals would be likely to make on their own in interview conditions.
- Allowing self de-selection if the methodology, style or content do not attract prospective participants.
- Enabling individuals to show their ability and willingness to work in groups, or for potential problems to be identified early.

Suggested processes include:

- A round of introductions with a little background.
- Forming buzz groups (see page 73) to report on what people want to get out of the course, and then the facilitator gives further information if it seems needed.
- Forming buzz groups on 'what do potential participants want to know about the course' and the facilitator gives the information requested:
  - Grouping areas of concern and addressing main issues
  - Brainstorming potential problems which people may encounter
  - If quality or evidence of previous work is necessary for admission, asking everyone to come with evidence ready to exhibit. Ensure that everyone exhibits their work and that all visit each other's and discuss it.

You will still need to be available afterwards to deal with individual queries and sometimes to follow up individuals who do not seem appropriate for the course.

26 Who does what?

When you have planned a workshop to meet particular aims and objectives and worked out how you will structure the material and time it all, there is an interesting check you can make on 'who does what?'

The problem is that when you are concentrating on the subject matter and the best way to help someone else understand it, you tend to plan in terms of what the facilitator will do at each stage and you can easily overlook the actual activity of the participants.

Make up a chart with columns for the programme, the facilitator and the participants as shown in Table 26.1.

Table 26.1 *Checking who does what*

Programme	Facilitator	Participants
9.00 Introductions	Introduce self	Introduce selves
9.10 Introduce subject	Talk, use OHP	Listen, watch
9.30 Demonstration	Demonstrate	Listen, watch
10.00 Go through theory	Talk, handouts	Listen, watch
10.30 Show video	Listen, watch	Listen, watch
11.00 Coffee break		

Fill in who does what, and you can see that what looked like an interesting and varied programme gave the facilitator lots of different activities but left the participants doing the same thing for the most part of two hours.

Once you have tried this, you will not need to make out the chart, but can test your programmes in your mind.

27 Room layout

Room layout makes a statement. When participants enter, they will immediately make all sorts of assumptions from their first impressions. If you decide what impression you would like to create, you have some chance of designing the arrangements to do that.

Consider the range of activities planned and make provision for them all—sitting, writing, moving into smaller groups, looking at visual aids, having coffee, getting to the doors, etc.

When you have arranged the room go outside and come in critically.

Seating arrangements

We once had to run a workshop in a coach. We learnt the following from this experience:

- That eye-contact is as important as everyone says it is
- That facilitating is difficult if you can't see over most of the participants and they are all standing in the only walking space
- That everyone is likely to talk at once if they can't see the facilitator
- That if they all sit down and can see the facilitator they can't see each other
- That the only person everyone can hear is the one with the microphone (good prospects for the power-hungry)
- That talking to your neighbour is preferable to listening to the microphone
- That group work is very dependent on seating arrangements

and a few other things . . .

Choices

Tables or no tables? Some workshop rooms are filled with tables, others contain just seats—and there is everything in between. Obviously, if participants need tables to work on (e.g. to write on), you are going to have to decide how best to place the tables as well as the chairs. However, if participants don't really need tables to write on, the workshop can at a stroke be made much less formal by pushing all the tables to the periphery of the room, and arranging just the chairs in a suitable way (e.g. circles or into a U-shape). Not having tables avoids participants 'hiding behind' them, and can make people more open and willing to discuss ideas.

If you have a room where the tables are small and easily moved there are a lot more choices as follows.

Traditional classroom layout

This is a lot like a coach (Fig. 27.1). If you want to be totally in control and the focus of attention, it is splendid (until the high spirits of the participants rise and very quickly remove your power). Lines of communication, when it works as planned, are from facilitator to each individual and back. Group work is possible in pairs without moving. It is also possible without too much disruption to turn pairs round to face other pairs and make fours.

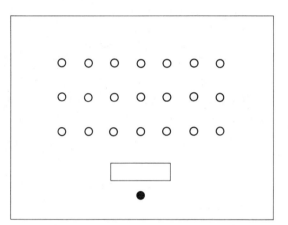

Figure 27.1   *A traditional classroom layout*

Cabaret style

This is a friendlier version of the classroom layout, in which tables are grouped to give a good view of the 'stage' but several participants sit around each table (Fig. 27.2). It allows everyone to see some other participants as well as the facilitator and it has groups already arranged.

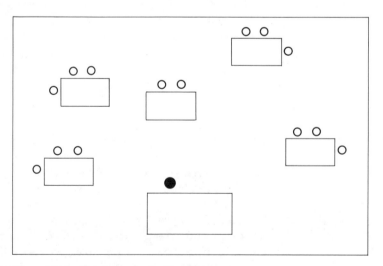

Figure 27.2   *One form of cabaret-style layout*

Of course, the tables don't need to be all set 'straight' as in our illustration—it can be even more interesting to have all the tables at different angles, so that each position in the room is a little unique. 'Cabaret' tables also make it possible to move into syndicate work without changing any furniture.

The boardroom This is useful if a long session is planned, in which everyone has lots of papers to manage and needs to see each other, but it gets out of hand if there are more than about 20 participants (Fig. 27.3). The best place for the facilitator depends on the width of the central table. It may be possible to have a hole in the middle in which you can wander around, if you don't mind being caged. It is also possible then to move participants with some coming into the hole to face others and work in groups.

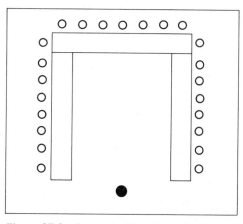

Figure 27.3 *One sort of boardroom layout*

Circles These are good with or without tables because they allow everyone to make contact with each other (Fig. 27.4). If you don't need tables it is better without if you plan to move into different sorts of groups. A U-shape may be better than a circle if the facilitator wants to remain in

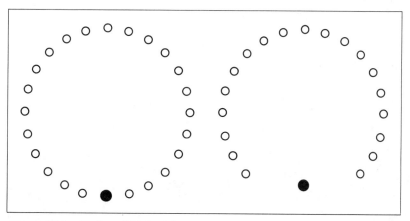

Figure 27.4 *Circle and U-shape layouts*

control of proceedings a little more or if visual aids are going to be in use.

Syndicates These can be formed at separate tables or areas in a big room if you want to have a lot of work in biggish groups yet bring everyone together sometimes. It is often useful, however, to have separate small rooms available for syndicate work. This can give participants a change of view, and can be a welcome relief, particularly at longer workshops. It is even worth trying to ensure that each participant has the opportunity to spend some time in each of several different syndicate rooms, rather than always go to the same one. Don't forget, however, that when syndicates are in separate rooms, it sometimes takes quite some time to get them all back for plenary sessions—there is always one syndicate that somehow manages to disappear altogether for a while (particularly with residential workshops run in hotels!).

Traditional lecture theatre This is probably the hardest room to work in with its ranked and fixed seating. If you find yourself running a workshop here, something has gone wrong with the planning! However, it is possible to encourage group work by having people turn round to form fours and even to move around to compare notes or present their findings from the central lion's pit! You might even see it as a challenge and aim to splatter it with flipcharts and post-it slips and take trips round the periphery to view the writings.

Outside The outdoors might be better than the wrong sort of room if the weather is fine enough. You might find a good space in pleasant surroundings and avoid the feeling of being cooped up inside and missing good weather. However, do make sure everyone is happy to go outside—it may be disastrous for hay-fever sufferers and those who hate wasps, and some may need shade from strong sun (we should be so lucky . . .). Outside can be a good place for syndicate work, but is likely to be less suitable for plenaries, as sound does not usually travel well in the open air.

28 Housekeeping—a checklist

Especially in extended workshops—such as residentials—your role of workshop facilitator may extend into many other areas. If things go wrong, it may not be your fault—but the whole workshop could suffer. There are many things to bear in mind, taking action when necessary. The following checklist is not intended to be exhaustive, but should alert you to the sort of things we have in mind:

Make announcements   'Before we start, can I tell you about a few domestic arrangements?' is a common beginning. Don't forget to mention the location of toilets and telephones. Mention when refreshment breaks will occur. On residential workshops, check whether anyone has problems with rooms.

Take responsibility for 'comfort'   This can include checking that the temperature suits everyone as far as possible, and that no participants are suffering from draughts (or noise from outside) coming in from open windows or doors. Participants who smoke will appreciate knowing where they may be allowed to do so—during breaks.

Make sure that the screen and flipcharts are visible to all participants without the projector getting in the way, and that participants are not having to sit 'looking sideways' for long periods of time.

Take refreshments seriously   Participants may be longing for that coffee break, so if the coffee is late in arriving, chase it up. Make sure that there is something for participants who don't drink coffee—or who like the decaffeinated variety. If a meal takes longer than planned, make it clear to everyone that the re-start time will be postponed to a known time, so no one feels they must bolt their dessert.

Tidy up   During breaks, throw away debris such as flipcharts and handouts no longer needed. Move any excess chairs and tables out of the way (e.g. when 16 people have turned up for a workshop planned for 20).

Know a person 'who can'   You can't be held responsible for every eventuality—but it is usually possible to find a person who can deal with it. In hotels, there is usually someone in overall charge of arrangements for workshops and conferences. Spend some time with such persons, letting them know what sort of workshop you are planning to run. Make sure you know them by name.

Cases and things   On residential workshops, announce in good time what time rooms are to be vacated, and where cases and coats may be stored thereafter. Similarly, ensure that there is somewhere for people to put their belongings before bedrooms become available.

29 Preconceived ideas and fears

Especially when the theme of a workshop may be found 'threatening' in some way to participants (e.g. when the aim may be to help them do something differently than they do in their day-to-day work), it is natural that participants will have preconceived ideas and fears. If you fail to acknowledge these ideas or fears, they will probably simmer on during the workshop, and possibly 'erupt' destructively later.

Getting them out in the open

A quick and thorough way of bringing preconceived ideas and fears out into the open is to ask participants to do a 'strengths, weaknesses, opportunities, threats' (SWOT) analysis (Fig. 29.1). This has the major advantages that it couples positive and negative things together.

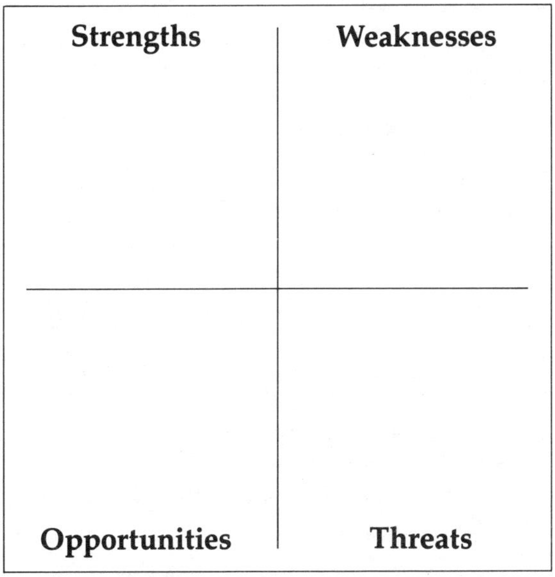

Strengths	Weaknesses
Opportunities	Threats

Figure 29.1 *Preparation for a SWOT analysis*

Participants can be asked to do the analysis individually, or in groups (where there is relative comfort of anonymity). They are issued with sheets (or flipcharts) with four boxes. The analysis can be applied to almost anything, with words such as: 'faced with the prospect of introducing . . . into your work, write down candidly your hopes and fears in the four categories: strengths, weaknesses, opportunities and threats'.

Putting them on the wall

Having got participants to bring their preconceived ideas and fears out into the open, it is often enough to simply keep them in sight. Most participants are satisfied that they had the opportunity to express these ideas and fears. It is also very useful for you as a facilitator to keep these ideas and fears in view—you can often link your suggestions to ideas that have already been expressed by participants, and you can look for ways of overcoming the problems and fears they may have expressed.

SWOT analysis can be turned into a way of establishing a contract with your participants, showing that you value their preconceived ideas, and that you will work towards solutions for their fears.

Defusing controversy

A useful way of exploring attitudes and support for different viewpoints is to facilitate workshop participants in having focused and one-to-one discussions on the controversial topic.

Share and compare: 'a line-up'

The first stage is to identify two participants who hold strong and preferably opposing viewpoints. You might need to prepare these individuals and gain their permission before beginning this exercise. Ask each of these participants to express their views to the whole group so that everyone can appreciate the different stances taken. Then ask these two people to stand at opposite ends of the room. Ask everyone else to put themselves between the two extremes, standing in a line in the place where they think their own viewpoint would fit. To check their position in the line they should briefly discuss their views on the topic with their neighbours and reposition themselves if necessary.

Once everyone is comfortably placed, number the line starting at one end and going to the middle (you need to know the total number of participants) then start again at one and continue to the other end of the line. It should look something like this:

1 2 3 4 5 6 7 8 9 10 11 12 13 1 2 3 4 5 6 7 8 9 10 11 12 13

Then ask everyone to find the person with the same number as themselves and pair up—this should ensure that the views held by each member of the pair are quite different. The pair then tell each other why they hold the views they do, five minutes each person, without interruption or discussion. When both have explained their views, they hold a discussion.

The line-up can be re-convened after the paired discussions to see if anyone wants to shift position, if anyone has changed views.

This process can enable a detailed discussion of a matter on which opinions are quite strongly held, allowing participants a chance to listen to other viewpoints and maybe change their own opinions.

30 Learning names

Introductions are always important at a workshop. On longer work-shops (lasting more than one day) and residentials, introductions are even more important so it is worth devoting more time to them. People generally feel more comfortable when they are referred to by name and when they are able to use the names of other participants. For this reason we have included a couple of activities to enable participants to learn the names of other participants.

Learning activity 1 Apart from helping the participants to learn each other's names, this first activity can help to break the ice and raise energy levels. It will also give a sense of achievement at an early stage.

- Ask how many members of the group have no difficulty learning other people's names. Explain that the aim of this activity is to help them to learn each other's names.
- Stand (or sit) with the participants in a circle so that each member of the group can see the face of everyone else in the group (Fig. 30.1).

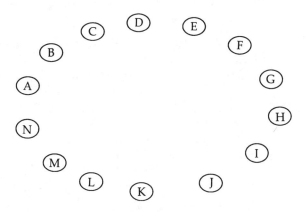

Figure 30.1 *Seating arrangements for a learning-names activity*

- Assuming that you are A, find out the name of the person, N, on your right. Then introduce him/her and yourself (loudly) to the person on your left, B, with the formula phrase: 'Hello, my name's . . . and I'd like to introduce you to my friend . . . .'
- B turns to C and says: 'Hello, my name's B and I'd like to introduce you to my friends A and N.'

- C turns to D and says: 'Hello, my name's C and I'd like to introduce you to my friends B, A and N.'

And so on round the group. (Remarkably, the only limit on the size of the group that this game can be used with seems to be determined by space rather than number of participants.)

People are invariably much more successful at this than they expect to be, so it raises confidence levels for subsequent workshop activities.

If you want to get even more from this activity you can conclude it with a plenary in which the following questions are addressed:

- Why was it important to see each other's faces?
- How did you feel about being located towards the beginning/end of the round? And how do you feel about that now?
- How did you feel before it was your turn?
- How did you feel after you had done your bit?
- After it was your turn did you continue to be involved? . . . Did you use this as an opportunity to learn the names of the other people here?
- Who gained most—those who went first or those who went last?
- How did you feel when someone couldn't remember your name?
- When someone couldn't remember your name did you want to help? Did you help? If so, how did you feel about that?
- If you were helped, how did you feel about that? From this, can you distinguish between rescuing someone and enabling someone to learn?
- What did you learn from this activity about how you learn?

Learning activity 2   This approach to learning names is simpler but it does not have quite the same learning potential.

- Ask the participants to stand in a circle.
- Take a soft object like a beach ball, a bean bag or a small cushion. The person with the 'soft object' throws it to someone whose name they know and at the same time calls out the recipient's name.
- That person then throws it someone whose name they know as they call out the name.
- Let the process continue until you are pretty sure that everyone knows the name of everyone else.
- Keep your awareness on who is not having the object thrown to them. When the object is thrown to you then use it as an opportunity to include such people.

This approach to learning names is less stressful than the first approach, as participants are only asked to identify the names that they have already learned.

31 Three icebreakers

Unstructured group task

Divide the participants into groups of about five. Give the groups 15 minutes to complete the following task:

Identify and assemble all the objects, data and ideas that you are likely to find useful to you throughout the rest of the workshop.

At the end of 15 minutes ask each group to present and explain what it has come up with. Possible discussion questions are:

- How did the group organize itself to conduct the task (e.g. with specializations or not?).
- How was this method chosen and how successful was it?
- What would you do differently when assigned another learning task as a group?

You could also ask the participants to form groups for groupwork and then explore the criteria they chose in selecting their group members.

Autographs 1

Ask each participant to take out a clean sheet of paper and a pen or pencil. Then announce that there will be a prize for whoever is first to collect everyone else's autograph on their sheet. This usually results in a lot of laughter and chaos. Have a prize such as a small box of chocolates ready for the winner.

Autographs 2

Using the sheet in Fig. 31.1, ask the participants to seek out fellow participants and if one of the items applies to them then sign the sheet in the spot provided. Only one spot should be signed even though more than one item applies. Possibly award a prize to the first person to get all the names of all the other participants on their sheet.

Seek out the other participants in this workshop and ask them to sign their name in one of the spaces below that applies to them.

Only one space should be signed by each person.

Sign here

Plays football	_____
Likes Mozart	_____
Is wearing green	_____
Belongs to a trade union	_____
Has children	_____
Has at least two grandchildren	_____
Hates cricket	_____
Is wearing earring(s)	_____
Likes black sausage	_____
Reads *The Guardian*	_____
Owns a cycle	_____
Speaks French	_____
Feels nervous	_____
Intends to take early retirement	_____
Has heard of Hank Wangford	_____
Skis	_____
Has attended at least two other workshops this year	_____
Plays a musical instrument	_____
Voted for Britain to enter the EEC	_____
Loves garlic	_____
Hates spinach	_____
Enjoys C and W music	_____

Figure 31.1 *Sample form for an icebreaking task*

32 Four things in common

This is an activity for longer residential workshops—three days or more—to help people get better acquainted. It is particularly useful when the participants will continue to work together after the residential.

Objectives
- To encourage each participant to make contact with each of the other participants.
- To discourage the formation of cliques by groups of participants who already know each other.

Ask the participants to find, over the space of the first two days of the residential, four things that they have in common. This gives them a reason to talk to all of the other participants. This is especially useful where the group comprises some people who already know each other and some who are 'newcomers'. Also, finding things in common is a way of developing empathy so that there is a significant team-building element to this activity.

On the morning of the third day of the residential, include a session in which each person shares one thing (the most interesting thing?) that they have found they have in common with each of the other participants.

This activity is constrained by the length of the residential and the number of participants. The shorter the residential and the larger the number of participants, the smaller must be the number of 'things in common' to be found.

Instead of setting this activity up to take place outside of the workshop sessions (during breaks and in the bar at the end the day) you could have a workshop session for this activity. You can constrain the choice of 'things in common'. For example, you could ask the participants to identify four things in common that they like, four things in common that they dislike, four things in common from their work experience, four things in common from their childhood and so on.

33 Ground-rules

Why have ground-rules?

Workshops need structure to work well. Agreeing ground-rules is a major way of constructing a 'contract' of behaviour at the start of a workshop.

Establishing ground-rules is a way of making clear what behaviour you would like of the participants. It also gives the participants an opportunity to make clear what behaviour they would like of you and of each other. Establishing ground-rules is an assertive thing to do.

Ground-rules make it less likely that those at the workshop will be disappointed and frustrated by the behaviour of others at the workshop. This enables participants to give their attention to the topic of the workshop rather than to behaviours that they do not like.

- Explain the rationale of having ground-rules. You can say that another name for ground-rules is a 'group contract'.
- Invite participants to suggest ground-rules. As facilitator you are also a participant so feel free to contribute any that you regard as important.
- Flipchart the results.

Establishing ground-rules

The most effective way to establish ground-rules is when the workshop participants suggest the ground-rules themselves. That way they feel more ownership of them. A good procedure for this is as follows. Ask each participant to spend five minutes making a list of possible ground-rules. Then ask participants to form groups of four to combine lists (this should take about 10 minutes). Finally, in the whole group, a full list is established. Alternatively, a quicker method is to use brainstorming. If there are some ground-rules that you regard as important and that don't emerge from this process, don't be afraid to suggest them yourself.

The next stage is to secure assent and ownership of the ground-rules. One way is to ask 'Is this agreed?' and ask for a response from each person. If you do this then don't assume that silence means assent. Ask the participants to say 'yes' or 'no' to each item, to raise their hands to signify agreement or to indicate agreement in some other positive way. If this seems too 'heavy', then you can use an explicit 'contracting out' policy by asking if there is 'any dissent' to each of the items. If you use this approach, make a point of checking out (at least in terms of eye contact) each of the participants. Leave any items that produce disagreement to the end for separate negotiation.

Establishing ground-rules can take up a lot of time. You may not have that time on, say, a one-day (or even a half-day) workshop. For short workshops you may wish to simply announce a few key ground-rules and check out for dissent.

Possibilities

Here are some possible ground-rules:

1 Smoking (no smoking? only at certain times? – only in certain places?)
2 Let the facilitator know if you are uncomfortable (heat, ventilation, etc.).
3 Don't 'put down' others at the workshop.
4 Respect the right to be heard—don't interrupt others when they are talking.
5 Respect each other's contributions.
6 It is OK to express feelings as well as thoughts and ideas about what happens at the workshop—'feelings are facts'.
7 Opting out: if you don't want to participate in any activity then it is OK to opt out. If you intend to do this then let the facilitator know clearly.
8 Confidentiality.
9 If you want the attention of the group raise your hand. If you see anyone else with their hand up then put your hand up too and stop talking.
10 'Own' your statements. Say 'I' rather than 'we', 'you', or 'one' when you really mean 'I'. This is easy to agree to but often hard to achieve in practice. It is helpful if the people at the workshop are vigilant.
11 It is the responsibility of each person at the workshop to get what they want from the workshop.
12 Punctuality.
13 New ground-rules can be added at any time.

34 Nominal group technique

Objectives
- To harvest the ideas of a group of people.
- To identify the strength of support within the group for the various ideas.
- To avoid the domination of the discussion by a single person or a small subgroup.

This is a versatile technique that combines elements of personal brainstorming with group evaluation.

1 Spend a few minutes introducing the nominal group technique and explaining the reasons for using it.
2 Identify an open-ended question. For example: In what ways could more cars be enabled to park on campus?
3 Ask the participants to individually spend a few minutes writing down about three to five brief suggestions.
4 Divide the participants into groups of five to ten. Give each group flipchart paper, Blu-tack and a marker pen.
5 Explain that the rest of the procedure is a group-based activity and the whole procedure will comprise the steps shown below (these can be flipcharted).

Step 1 *Group leader*
Decide on a group leader to record ideas on the flipchart.

Step 2 *Round-robin recording of ideas*
The leader goes round the group and collects one idea from each person—writes them on the flipchart so that they can all be seen. There is no discussion, elaboration or justification of ideas at this stage. There is no need to reach a consensus on these. For example, if there is disagreement, two contradictory comments can be included on the list.

Step 3 *Clarification of each idea*
The group leader checks that each idea is understood by all group members.

Step 4 *Voting*
Individually, evaluate the ideas, giving a 5 rating for the most important, 4 for the next most important, 3 for the next most important and so on. Then the leader collects in the votes for each of the items and ranks the items according to the number of 'votes' secured.

Step 5 *Report back*
The group leader reports back on group results.

This process sounds more complicated than it is. Groups rarely experience any difficulty with it. It has many uses such as identifying the most important issues for syndicate groupwork, allowing participants to compare their own judgements about the most important issues with those of others, evaluating a workshop and so on.

Variations This process can be carried out with the whole group with the facilitator acting as the group leader.

An additional stage that can be included is to compute the raw scores for each item into a figure for 'percentage of maximum possible'. An item would get 100 per cent if all the group members gave it five votes. So the actual percentage score for an item will be 100 times the actual number of votes secured divided by five times the number in the group.

A simpler voting method is to give each person five 'votes' to give to the five items felt to be most important.

Votes can be collected in all sorts of different ways, including:

- Asking each participant to shout his/her 'score' and writing all the scores on a flipchart.
- Giving all participants some coloured sticky dots (e.g. red for first choice, blue for second choice, and so on) and letting them stick their dots beside the flipcharted items.

35 Brainstorming

Group techniques

Brainstorming is a way to generate a large number of useful ideas on any subject or problem by suspending criticism, judgement and evaluation. It is also useful to develop groupwork skills by introducing a group technique for creative problem solving. It encourages cooperative and collaborative behaviour. Brainstorming is so useful that it is worth spending a little time 'teaching' it and practising it. Here is a way of approaching this.

First, say to the group: 'Imagine that you are cast ashore on a desert island, naked and with only one manufactured object: a belt. Using your wildest imaginations think of as many uses as possible for the belt.'

State the following rules:

- No comment, criticism, judgement or evaluation during the brainstorming phase.
- As many ideas as possible—the objective is quantity not quality.
- The wildest ideas possible.
- Build upon each other's ideas.

Write down every idea on a flipchart, blackboard or a sheet of newsprint, without comment, discarding nothing. You can also put in ideas (thus becoming a contributing member of the group).

After the ideas have stopped coming (this can be checked by doing a 'round'—see below), point to each idea, and ask how many people think it has possibilities. Erase ones that attract no 'votes' at all. Discuss the remaining ones in detail, and eventually choose a 'best one' (by acclaim or by voting).

The second stage is to form groups of about six participants each. Each group is to select a secretary to record the ideas. Give the groups three minutes to brainstorm uses of a Coca-Cola bottle on a desert island (instead of a belt).

Finally, lead a discussion of brainstorming as an approach to creative problem solving.

Variations

1 Other objects can be used in the problem such as a rope, a shoe, an oar, an economics textbook, a brick, etc.
2 Instead of allowing participants to call out ideas ('free-for-all'), an alternative procedure is to use 'rounds'. In a 'round' each person in

the group contributes an idea or says 'pass'. Or the two approaches can be combined: start off with a free-for-all and when the flow of ideas becomes thin do a few rounds to finish.

3 In the second stage of the brainstorming exercise, count the total number of ideas after the ideas-generating phase and announce the total for each group. Then give the teams a few minutes to reach a group decision about which are their five most original ideas (i.e. ones that the other teams will not have). Each team then reads out the five that they have chosen. Give points for any ideas which have not been thought of by any other team.

4 This exercise may be done as a preliminary to a problem-solving session involving a 'real' problem (see page 66 for some suggestions).

Possible discussion questions

How could two or more of the ideas generated be used in combination?

In this exercise a large amount of creativity was released by suspending criticism, evaluation or judgement—so what is the role of criticism, evaluation and judgement in problem solving?

What conditions are favourable to creativity? (In what conditions/situations do you feel most creative?)

Using brainstorming to build scenarios

This technique works well in workshops when all participants are from one organization or where they have a common interest which they want to protect and guide into the future. It is particularly good for helping individuals to think more widely about how their actions affect the future, how today's solution may be tomorrow's problem. It can encourage participants to consider methods of planning for the future and to be more aware of the consequences of their own actions.

There are many ways of using scenarios either by building them with the group or by presenting the group with a scenario as a problem.

One way of building with the group is to ask them to brainstorm a list of things that could affect their organization or field of interest in the future. Once the list is fairly full, divide it among subgroups and ask each group to describe the likely effect on the organization or field of interest if each of the possible developments actually happened.

Come back together to present these projections and collate them on a new flipchart.

Then focus on how the organization or field of interest could prepare for each eventuality. This could be done as a whole group or in smaller subgroups, depending on the size of the whole group and the particular interests of individuals—this can be an opportunity for people with similar interests or responsibilities to compare plans.

The results of these discussions are shared with the whole group and the implications discussed. Possible directions are considerations of planning processes, training plans, communications within the organization, monitoring of the environment and change, etc.

Another way of using scenarios is to give the workshop participants a particular scenario and ask them to say what they would do—either as individuals or to discuss it in groups. This can work very strongly if the participants have common concerns—for example, a group of people from the health and social services can be faced with a particular social crisis, or a group of managers with a business crisis. Other examples of this use of scenarios are in the emergency services where sessions are held to closely resemble real crisis situations.

The process can be very strong if individuals can act in something like their normal roles, then discuss the effect of their choice of action. The debriefing is very important to capturing the learning in these situations, and sufficient time should be allowed to really explore the implications in whatever way is appropriate for the particular group of participants.

Sample brainstorming topics

Here is a list of topics which can be used for 'brainstorming' during induction into higher education:

1 What activities can you do during your period at college when you are not studying?
2 What activities can help you learn in addition to attending classes or reading?
3 How do you cope with a poor lecturer?
4 How do you know when you have done something well? (i.e. what possible sources of feedback can you think of?)
5 What are the possible problems of transition into higher education?
6 What are the good aspects of transition into higher education?
7 What are the bad aspects of transition into higher education?
8 What makes an effective member of a group?
9 What is it that makes a 'supportive' group supportive?
10 What are the possible improvements to the induction programme for next year?
11 How do you know when you are learning effectively?
12 What are the possible difficulties in adjusting to studying at the institution?
13 What constitutes a good 'climate' for learning?
14 What new skills would be helpful for living and studying at the institution?
15 What sources of stress could be encountered in the transition into higher education?
16 What can you do when the book that you have been recommended is not in the library?
17 When you are working on a group assignment, how can you tell if your group is not working well?
18 The transition into higher education, like other transitions, involves taking on of new things and 'letting go' of some other things. What things might it involve letting go of?

19 What makes a good seminar?
20 What makes a 'good' tutor?
21 What makes a 'bad' tutor?
22 What are tutors really like?
23 What makes a 'good' student?
24 What makes a 'bad' student?
25 What are students really like?
26 What makes for enjoyable learning?
27 What study skills would it be good to have?
28 Suppose that you are dissatisfied with your skills in taking notes in lectures and you feel that you need some help with this. What resources are available to you?

36 Ownership and how we learn

We hope our participants are going to learn something at our workshops. It is interesting for them—and us—to find out more about how they learn.

Objectives
- To give participants an exercise that they can all do—whatever their past experience.
- To give you the chance to build your workshop around the way your participants learn.
- To allow participants to feel a stronger sense of ownership of the way the workshop is run, and the ways they contribute to it.

How do you learn?
The following simple exercise can be done in less than 10 minutes.
- Ask participants to jot down privately something they know they are good at (this should take less than a minute).
- Ask them to write on a Post-it slip a few words explaining how they became good at whatever it is (this takes two or three minutes).
- Ask them to stick their Post-it slips with details of how they learned (not what they became good at) on a wall of the room, or a flipchart, (two minutes).
- Allow them a minute or two to compare their ways of learning, and discuss the common threads that always emerge from this exercise.

It seems to matter little what participants choose to think about in terms of the skill they became good at. The processes always include the following:

- practice
- learning by doing
- learning by mistakes

and relatively few references to 'being taught'.

We have given two examples of this exercise—with widely different participant groups. The exercise naturally attracts some flippancy—but this is quite useful, as even so the intended effect is usually achieved.

What makes you feel good
This is a similar sort of exercise to the one described above, except that this time participants are asked to:

- Think of something they feel good about.
- Write a few words on a Post-it, justifying the positive feeling.

Most participants come up with phrases such as 'feedback', 'other people's reactions'—in other words, positive learning experiences depend not only on learning by doing, but also on feedback.

Example 1 The following set of ways people learn was drawn from some higher education lecturers near the start of a workshop on working with large student groups:

- practice, natural talent, interest, enjoyment
- played a lot; read about the game, watched top-class players
- studying books and watching TV programmes
- discussing with others interested and specialists
- experimentation
- natural aptitude, parental encouragement, opportunity to practise by playing
- enjoyable practice, good coaching and facilities
- mixing with people, attending lots of lectures, attending lots of meetings
- practising regularly, taking breaks from time to time to sit back and review progress; asking others for criticism; public performances
- primary school practice, I like the activity
- observing others, practice, experience, learning from others' mistakes
- natural ability, training and practice
- numerous visits from relatives coming for meals (i.e. practice)
- by regular practice, enjoyment of activity
- practice over a long period, learning from others
- discussion and practice with an experienced practitioner; regular practice, variety of experience
- practice, reading about it, trial and error

The word practice had not been mentioned at all in the task briefing! This is the common thread in most participants' responses. Even thought the actual content of the things people had become good at were likely to cover a wide range of talent and ability, the means to the end remains similar—practice and experience.

Ownership of learning Many of the items in this book are about helping workshop participants to contribute actively to workshops, and enabling them to express their expectations, views, reservations, anxieties, and learning outcomes. Exercises on 'how people learn' at the beginning of a workshop allow participants to see how you intend to take their own ways of learning into account during the workshop. The more it is possible to delegate control to participants (while still ensuring that the workshop is productive and focused), the more positive will be their feelings about what they are learning, and the deeper their learning will be.

The two factors which contribute most to a feeling of ownership are:

- Activity-based workshops—learning by doing.
- Abundance of feedback—from each other and from facilitators.

Example 2   A large group of students gave a memorable set of ways of becoming good at something—this time matching the skills to the processes—including the following:

Driving	Lessons, test, practice
Playing the piano	Practice, lessons
Sex	Practice, pleasure, pain
Dancing	Practice, lessons, experience
Gardening	Experience, reading about it, talking and listening to gardeners
Painting	Taught techniques, then practice and experimentation
Essays	Practice
Table tennis	Taught, practice, time, experience, sticking with it, endeavour
Cooking	Practice, necessity, interest
Acting	Practice, taught techniques by tutor, involving myself in pantomimes
Driving	Taking lessons, passing a test, driving daily, continuing to learn
Driving	Perseverance, determination, good teaching, patience, bribing examiner!
Embroidery	Taught basics, practice and own mistakes
Painting	Practice, natural ability
Playing clarinet	Practice, making mistakes, help from others, books, threats
Swimming	Starting young, practice, taking tests
Swimming	Practice, enjoyment
Playing flute	Practice, passing exams, tutoring
Drinking beer	Extended practice, socializing
Sex	Practice, pain, pleasure and struggle and hard work
Tennis	Practice, hard work
Playing pool	Practice, interest, advice, watching others
Wallpapering	Watching somebody qualified
Mixing concrete	By trial and error after being shown how to do it
Catering for 90	Practice (no choice—dropped in at deep end)
Making model aircraft	Practice
Drawing	Practice, looking at mistakes, not being afraid to make mistakes, experimenting, analysing mistakes
Ballet	Practice, lessons, good teacher, enthusiastic at progress
Drawing	Practice, lessons, encouragement

Talking	Practice, discussions with other people
Sewing	Being taught, practice, enjoying doing it so practising more

A further common thread that can be inferred from many of the students' responses above is that there is a strong connection between becoming confident and successful learning.

37 Good and bad learning experiences

Objectives
- To identify characteristics that contribute to a good learning experience.
- To encourage participants to take more responsibility for their own learning.

Ask each participant to recall a really good learning experience and a bad learning experience. Explain that this may have been in an academic context or in a non-academic context (it may be helpful to ask the group to give examples of learning in a non-academic context).

Ask each participant to compare their experiences with those of a partner and identify what elements their good learning experiences had in common and what elements their bad learning experiences had in common.

Ask each pair to join another pair and produce a combined list of characteristics associated with a good learning experience and with a bad learning experience. Ask each group of four to agree on a spokesperson who will report to the rest of the class the findings of the group.

Go round each group asking for one characteristic of a good learning experience and one characteristic of a bad learning experience, and flipchart these. Continue until all of the characteristics have been listed.

Possible discussion questions
- What have the characteristics of a good learning experience got in common? And the characteristics of a bad learning experience?
- What differences in attitude make for a good learning experience? And a bad learning experience?
- Which of the identified characteristics do the participants have control over and which are outside their control?

Variations
After the plenary, discuss in groups how each person could go about generating the characteristics of a good learning experience—each group flipcharts its conclusions. This to be followed by a report-back by each of the groups.

38 Buzz groups

A buzz group is a very small group (two to four people) who discuss a point or a problem for a short period (two to ten minutes). Buzz groups are a good way of getting the immediate reaction of the group to something. They are also a good way of breaking up a lecture. And they can be used to generate energy when the group is flagging.

Ask the participants to form small groups of two, three or four by simply turning to those nearest them to discuss their reaction to whatever it is that you want them to discuss. You might, for example, ask them to check out their understanding so far. You could ask them to discuss the most important thing that they learned from the previous day's session. You could ask them to discuss the relevance of the last session to their activities at work. Another good use of buzz groups is to ask the participants to identify any questions about the session so far.

There is no reason why you could not have a quick buzz group session quite frequently. But if you do, then make sure that you vary the questions and activities for the buzz groups. They will get bored if you always ask them to do the same thing.

You can ask a few buzz groups to report back to pick up the 'flavour' of the discussion and give you some feedback. Another way of using a buzz group session is to use it as the basis of a brief discussion with the larger group.

Remember that buzz groups are so-named because they generate a lot of noisy 'buzz' when you use them. Don't be surprised or alarmed at the sudden increase in the noise level.

Buzz groups work well for us when:
- The task or topic is easily understood
- The discussion does not require too much thought

Some of the times it is helpful to use them are when:
- You want everyone to have a chance to talk a little
- You want to change focus from previous work
- You want a change of atmosphere
- You have forgotten what you meant to do next and need to find your notes (use a topic like 'What have you learnt so far?')
- You want to wake everyone up
- You want to get a lively discussion started and need to develop some opinions first

Even if the furniture is difficult to move, this is a good way of helping participants interact with each other. Its only real problem is that people like doing it and find it interesting. It can be very difficult to quieten them down and get them to listen to you again . . . although you could try flicking the lights on and off!

Warning: Ending a buzz group session is not always easy!

39 Square-root groups

Participants get bored by repetition of workshop processes. Variety makes workshops more enjoyable and facilitates learning. For this reason it is a good idea to develop variations on the more powerful and versatile processes. One such process is the syndicate group (where the participants form groups, discuss an issue or work on some task and then report back to the rest of the participants (see 'syndicate groups'). 'Square-root groups' is a variation that removes the need for report-back presentations to the whole group.

- Explain that instead of choosing a spokesperson to report back the group's discussion, all the members of the group will be reporting back.
- Form groups such that the number of members in each is the square root of the total number of participants (or as close as you can get to it).
- After the initial group activity, form new groups in which each new group is made up of members of different original groups.
- One way of doing this is to number off the workshop participants at the outset in groups of, say, five. Then, at the subsequent round, say 'now all the ones form one group, and all the twos form a second group and so on'.
- The brief for the new groups is to compare notes on the discussion and conclusions reached by each of the original groups.

This is particularly suitable for a situation in which each of the groups has been working on the same (or similar) tasks. In this case the conventional report-back presentations to all the participants can be repetitive and thereby become tedious.

40 Owning objectives

Teachers are well aware of how much they learn when they plan sessions on topics to teach other people—i.e. one of the best ways to learn is to teach. This idea comes from that basis, and attempts to share with workshop participants some of the advantages of being involved in planning learning.

In planning workshops it is usual to decide overall aims and objectives before subsequent detailed planning. In order to do this, it is necessary to have a wide view of the subject and to be able to think strategically about how to package it for a learning experience. This is an important stage in getting to grips with the whole subject. Here is an example of how we shared this with our workshop participants so that they were involved in the learning arising from the planning experience.

1 The workshop was about how to improve written and verbal presentations, and all participants had some experience of the area of work and a perceived need to improve in some way. All were sent a package of material before the workshop including a lot of quotations referring to disastrous presentations, problems in presentations, some successes, some typical problem areas, etc.

2 The facilitators prepared probable content areas and the sorts of materials and processes that would help people to learn more about them. The workshop publicity did not state objectives, but rather areas that the workshop would address. The programme was outlined to address the areas mentioned but with considerable flexibility and with several alternative approaches.

3 Immediately after introducing people at the workshop, participants were asked to work in small groups using the pre-workshop material distributed. Their task was to draw up objectives for the workshop in the light of issues raised by the material.

4 Each group presented their objectives to the whole group and these were discussed in terms of arriving at ones of core importance. Individuals were asked to consider whether these objectives then appeared appropriate to meet individual needs and further discussion modified them as necessary.

5 The objectives were then displayed on the wall, and the facilitators huddled through coffee time to focus the programme to allow the objectives to be met. This meant that the facilitators were constantly juggling the available materials and processes to fit the perceived needs.

Arriving at objectives like this is a way of clarifying expectations while beginning to get to grips with the problems, and can help participants to be more aware of their individual needs and how to plan for their own learning.

41 Keeping a learning log

Residentials provide an opportunity for out-of-session activities. One such activity is to ask the participants to keep a log or journal of what they learn. This is particularly important when the workshop contains little formal input by way of presented information.

Objectives
- To cause the participants to reflect on the significance to them of the workshop experiences.
- To help the participants to become aware and acknowledge what they have learned.
- To give the participants a permanent record of their learning.

Distribute a small book titled 'learning log' to each of the participants. This makes it clear that the 'learning log' is an integral part of the workshop and not an optional extra.

Offer guidance as to what the participants might include in their journal. This will be something along the following lines:

The purpose of the learning log is for participants to pick out and record the most personally significant experiences on a particular day and record what they learned from the experience.

This will involve reflecting on:

- *what experience during the day was most significant to you personally*
- *why this was personally significant*
- *what you learned from it*
- *any actions you propose to take as a result*

Of course, you need not restrict yourself to just one experience.

You can also use the journal to record other thoughts, ideas, insights and feelings. This may include reflections on what worked and what didn't work (and why) and ideas for possible improvements. It may include reflections on the relevance of workshop experiences to activities and experiences outside of the workshop.

Set aside a period (at least an hour) towards the end of each day for completion of the journal, and have this period listed as such in the workshop programme. This too gives a signal about the importance that you attach to the activity.

On the penultimate day of the workshop suggest to participants that they spend some time that evening reviewing what they have written in their learning logs.

42 Idea-writing

This is a very productive group process that involves the participants working in parallel. It focuses on precisely what the participants wish to know—without the intermediation of the facilitator. Most of the participants will not have encountered this process before, so it has the merit of novelty and can contribute to variety in workshop processes.

- Ask participants to form small groups (of about four or five).
- Each participant takes an idea-writing sheet (an example is shown in Fig. 42.1). Participants then:
  - Write their names in the spaces provided.
  - Each write an open question—or statement on which they want comments. (You may want to suggest to the participants that they try to phrase their question using the stem 'How to . . .'. You may also wish to suggest that the value of the responses is likely to depend upon the importance of the issue to participants in general.)
  - Write their own responses to their own questions or statements.

Idea-writing sheet

Name: ....

My question or statement:

My own comments:

Your comments please:

Figure 42.1 A sample idea-writing sheet

- Participants then write their responses to what is written on each other's sheets. These first three stages can be simply explained by use of an acetate or flipchart (see Fig. 42.2).

---

1 Form small groups (of about four or five)

2 Each person takes idea-writing sheet and:

- Write your name in space provided
- Write an open question (or statement on which you want comments)
- Write your own response to your question or comment.

3 Each group member writes response to what is written on each other's sheets.

4 • Each group member reads what is on his/her sheet.
- Group then clarifies and discusses the ideas that have emerged.
- (Group summarizes discussion on flipchart for plenary—optional.)

Figure 42.2 *Sample acetate or flipchart for collecting responses*

- Explain the following 'rules':
  - The process should be done silently (otherwise this intrudes on the space of other group members).
  - Spelling is not important, style is not important, grammar is not important but legibility *is* important.
  - The writing phase should be completed in about 20–30 minutes.
  - Agree on a group leader (whose job is to see that the group follows the steps).
  - In the responses, it is OK to offer advice, solutions, suggestions, to qualify and criticize what others have written (the contributions are anonymous).

For a suggested briefing flipchart, see Fig. 42.3.

- Each group member reads what is on his/her sheet and then the group clarifies and discusses the ideas that have emerged.

Because most of the work in this process is silent writing, it is a good process to use when you judge the participants need some quiet time. It also happens to be a good after-lunch activity as, although it doesn't involve participants in much activity, it does require energetic concentration.

Variations Each group can summarize the discussion on a flipchart for the plenary.

Ground-rules for idea-writing

1 The process should be done silently (otherwise this intrudes on the space of other group members)

2 Spelling is not important.
   Style is not important.
   Grammar is not important.
   LEGIBILITY is important.

3 Writing phase should be completed in about 20–30 minutes.

4 Agree on a group leader (whose job is to see that the group follows the steps and the ground-rules).

5 Responses—it's OK to offer advice, solutions, suggestions, qualify and criticize what others have written (the contributions are anonymous).

Figure 42.3   A suggested briefing flipchart

43 Flipchart wallpaper

Objectives
- To help the participants become aware of the work that has been done at the workshop.
- To help to create an environment where the participants are aware that their work is valued.
- To reinforce some of the learning of the workshop.

Over the course of the workshop, lots of sheets of flipchart paper are likely to be used. They may contain, for example, statements of objectives for the workshop by the facilitators and by the participants, ground-rules, report-backs from syndicate groups, and flipcharts produced as part of exercises by individual participants.

Instead of either discarding these or leaving the 'owners' to dispose of them as they wish, fix them to the walls with Blu-tack. When all the wall space is used up, replace the 'oldest' flipchart sheets with the ones newly produced, leaving up key ones that have enduring value within the workshop—such as the workshop ground-rules and participants' objectives for the workshop.

Using Blu-tack to fix the flipchart sheets to the walls ensures that they can be removed after the workshop without damaging the walls.

Variations   At the end of the workshop type up the contents of flipcharts produced during the workshop and circulate to the participants. You will probably want to be selective in doing this. Some flipcharts clearly have little value outside the context in which they were produced and it is usually not possible to do much with pictures produced by the participants. These can simply be left with the 'owners' to do with as they wish.

44 Non-participant observers

This is an idea to help participants to appreciate the value of communicating their purpose effectively, and to get feedback on their ideas. It is most useful towards the end of a workshop—at the action planning stage. More particularly, it is useful at the point where each person has an objective that they intend to pursue after the workshop.

- Ask participants to each write their objective on a flipchart as clearly and precisely as they can. (An alternative is to ask them to prepare two-minute presentations.)
- Then ask them to form small groups (in our experience four or five works best). Within each group one person is to display their flipcharted objective. The rest of the group are then to discuss for 15 minutes how he or she could go about achieving the objective while the 'owner' of the objective remains a non-participant observer.
- Encourage the non-participant observers to make notes during the session but give strict instructions to them not to speak at all while they are in that role.
- After the first round the groups repeat the process until all the group members have acted in the role of non-participant observer. At this point, all the participants reassemble as a full group and the plenary takes the form of a round of: 'One thing that I learned from that exercise' or 'One thing that I'm going to do as a result of that'.

Sometimes the group get hold of the wrong end of the stick entirely. This is a frustrating experience for the non-participant observer but it is not a wasted experience as it indicates that their objective was not clearly or precisely formulated. It is necessary to be very clear that the non-participant observer must not speak, as there is great pressure to 'put the group straight', correct misunderstandings or take issue with comments.

45 Free-range eggs

'Getting started' is often the most demanding part of any task, including the task of brainstorming ideas. At workshops, individual and syndicate tasks alike often begin with a brainstorming episode and benefit from starting quickly, rather than from thinking about the tasks and chatting about them for ages.

Objectives
- To increase the efficiency with which individuals—and syndicates—get down to 'starting-from-scratch' tasks.
- To enhance creative thinking, and increase the range of ideas generated by workshop participants.
- To provide participants with a general technique for 'getting started' on things, that they can take away from the workshop as a useful skill.

Individual free-range egg laying

1 Ask each participant to take a blank sheet, and draw 'an egg' approximately real size in the middle of the sheet (Fig. 45.1a). (For some strange reason, people find it much easier to draw 'an egg' than 'a circle about two inches in diameter'!)

2 Agree two or three key words to go 'in' the eggs (Fig. 45.1b). These words can be the gist of the question or topic to be creatively brainstormed.

3 Ask participants individually to quietly 'brainstorm' ideas relating to the topic, drawing a 'spoke' radiating out from the egg for each new idea, and adding just a word or two at the end of each spoke (Fig. 45.1c). Explain that each point must relate directly to the words in the egg (to maintain relevance to the task), but that all ideas—good and bad—should be written down (in other words 'free-ranging ideas').

4 Ask participants to look at the collection of points they have generated, and decide which is the most important point (or which would be the most logical first point), and write 1 beside it. Ask participants to continue prioritizing or ordering the points around their 'eggs' (Fig. 45.2).

5 Then collect the ideas from all participants—e.g. by asking each in turn for their 'most important point', making a 'master-egg' on a flipchart, then asking each for their 'next-most important point' and so on until no more interesting or important points remain.

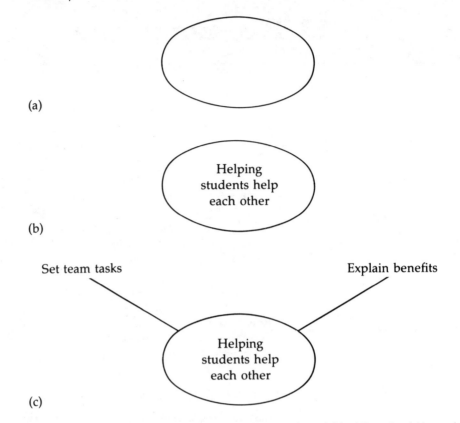

Figure 45.1   *(a) drawing an egg, (b) agreeing key words, and (c) adding related ideas*

Variations   *Battery eggs*   The same technique used by syndicates instead of individuals.

Poached eggs   Individuals are encouraged to look over each other's shoulders, and 'cheat'.

Hard-boiled eggs   The sort produced by experienced participants who know the topic backwards.

Pickled eggs   Produced at residential workshops where the technique may be extended to syndicate work in the bar late in the evening.

Omelettes   Produced when three of four participants take their 'eggs' into a syndicate task to produce a master-version.

Egg-on-face   Special use of the technique to predict all the things that could possibly go wrong with a course of action.

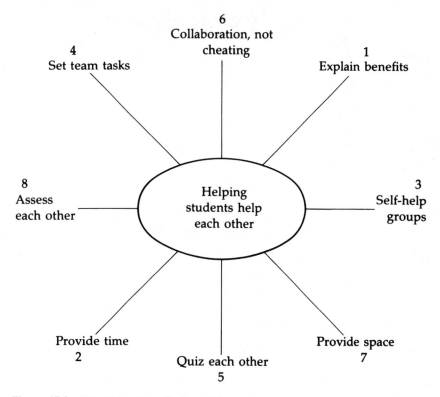

Figure 45.2   Prioritizing the collection of ideas

46 'Pyramiding' or 'snowballing'

These terms are used for processes whereby information or ideas are gathered from participants at a workshop, where they start working individually or in pairs, then continue in fours, then larger groups. These processes are also useful for helping participants get to know each other.

Stage 1
Participants are set a task which they all work on for a few minutes individually. The task can be almost anything that involves jotting a few notes or ideas down on paper.

Stage 2
Participants are then put into pairs, and asked to take the task a little further (possibly being given some additional information or resources to help them).

Stage 3
The pairs are regrouped into quartets, and asked to process the information brought to each quartet by the two pairs.

Stage 4
Quartets are combined into 'eights' or 'twelves', and asked to further develop the information or ideas, usually to a stage where the group prepares to report back to the whole workshop.

Advantages of pyramiding or snowballing include:

- Allowing everyone with ideas or information to contribute to the work which leads to the eventual report-back, thus establishing a feeling of participant ownership of ideas.
- Minimizing the embarrassment of participants without relevant experience or knowledge, as they can assist in the development of other people's ideas and information in the later stages.

Example   *Stage 1*   Individually, brainstorm features of a 'good' presentation.

Stage 2   In pairs, shortlist five key features, and put them in order of priority.

Stage 3   In fours, refine the list of the top five features, clarify the wording.

Stage 4   In eights, prepare an acetate showing the most important features of a good presentation, and give each feature a 'score' out of 30 to reflect its importance.

47 Six thinking gloves

Much has been written about 'learning styles' and 'approaches to thinking'. It seems likely that when tasks are approached in several different ways, there is an increased possibility of innovative and interesting solutions to problems. The following method can be used to increase the quality and interest of problem-solving activities at workshops, and to encourage participants to play with new approaches to problem solving.

This technique involves participants role-playing approaches they may not instinctively have chosen for themselves. It can be applied to problem solving, action planning, and any other situations where you may wish participants to come up with ways of tackling a situation, or ways of implementing a development. For example, participants can apply the method to tasks such as 'how mature students can get more out of higher education' or 'ways of improving time-management'.

There are several ways of dividing the 'six thinking gloves' among participants, including:

- Explain each of the six thinking gloves, then let each participant choose which to 'wear'.
- Explain each of the six thinking gloves, then let each of six syndicates self-select to use one of the approaches.
- Divide participants into six syndicates, then allocate to each syndicate its 'thinking glove'.

1   The research and observation glove
Observe and question people, then choose a course of action based on your observations.

2   The many-fingered glove
Work out several different ways of approaching the task, then modify and improve the one which seems most promising.

3   The firmly pointed glove

Fix your direction firmly, then concentrate on a single-minded, thorough approach to solving the problem in this direction.

4   The experiential glove

Work out an approach based on things that have worked in the past, and avoiding things that have not worked in the past.

5   The one-finger-at-a-time glove

Work out the approach one step at a time, but remain flexible to reconsider each successive step as you come to it.

6   The playful glove

Play with the ideas freely, and develop what turns up.

Multiplying the benefits   Having briefed different people (or different groups) to apply each of the six processes above, bring all the ideas together in a plenary session.

Variations   Ask teams to apply *two* of the approaches, and come up with hybrid solutions or plans.

48 The Zeigarnik effect

Here is a story that may possibly be true. When the famous psychologist Kurt Lewin was a young professor in Berlin he used to meet with students and young colleagues at a coffee-house. Lewin was impressed by how the waiter managed to keep track of the bill total for hours. On one occasion, some minutes after paying, he asked the waiter to recall the bill total and the waiter was unable to do so. Lewin's explanation for this is that the completion of the task led to extinction of the memory.

One of the students present on that occasion was Bluma Zeigarnik, who subsequently demonstrated experimentally that completed tasks are remembered less well than interrupted tasks. This phenomenon is now known as the Zeigarnik effect.

This may be one reason why unfinished tasks call out for completion—so that conscious awareness can be released for other current activities.

Question   What has all this got to do with residential workshops?

Answer   One way to sustain energy levels overnight at a residential is to start a long task late in the day—to be completed the next day. You might, for example, set up a syndicate group activity after dinner with the report-backs to take place on the following morning.

49 Review and preview sessions

Experienced lecturers often give the following advice: start by saying what you are going to say, say it and end by saying what you have said. In the context of a workshop, previews and reviews serve similar roles to 'saying what you are going to say' and 'saying what you have said'.

'Reviewing and previewing' help participants to know 'where they are' in the programme. It helps them to recognize and acknowledge their own learning. And it can help to put them into the right mental and emotional state for more learning.

It is important to preview the workshop at the start. This serves to align the expectations of the participants and those of the facilitator(s). It also provides the participants with an opportunity to negotiate changes from the programme that you have planned.

After that, we recommend frequent reviews and previews. The longer the workshop the more important are reviews and previews. On a workshop lasting several days we would normally start each new day with a review of the previous day and a quick preview of the new day.

A good way of reviewing the previous day is to do a round of 'one significant thing that I learned yesterday'. Ask the participants to spend a minute re-running the previous day in their minds and identifying learning points (if they wish to jot down a note of them that is fine). When someone is ready to volunteer their contribution then move sequentially round the other participants in order that they may each share a learning point. The combined responses will be a good summary of the significant issues that were learned and the process will have taken the participants' consciousness back to where they were the previous day. A 'round' like this also raises energy levels.

We suggest that as facilitator you join in the round when it comes to your turn and contribute something that you learned from the workshop the previous day; enthusiastic participation by you encourages enthusiastic participation by the other workshop members.

After the review you could ask 'Is there anything left over from yesterday?' And after dealing with any issues that result from that you are ready to give a brief preview of the new day.

We have said that reviews and previews are more important on longer workshops (including residentials). For a one-day workshop, a brief review and preview session is a useful way of starting the afternoon. For workshops that are shorter than one day, their value is more questionable.

50 Using overhead projectors

The overhead projector is one of the most useful tools for displaying ideas and information—but it can be infuriating to participants if it is not used well.

Placing the projector

It is best if participants can be as near as possible to a semi-circular 'orbit', with the screen at not too great an angle to any participant. Play around with the furniture in the room to maximize the number of participants who can see the screen easily. Remember that the participants who look most directly at the screen may be looking at the projector as well, and try to ensure that the images on the screen are high enough up so that the projector head does not have them bobbing and weaving! Luxuriate in an elevated, angled screen when you have the chance.

Figures 50.1 to 50.3 show three different ways of placing a projector, maintaining a U-shape of participants (so they can all see each other).

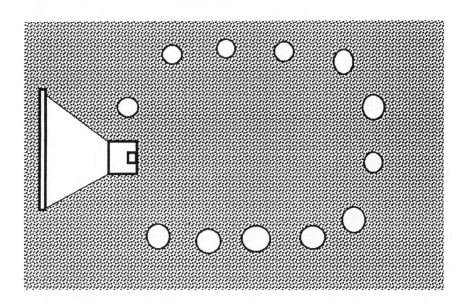

Figure 50.1 *Screen placed on the short wall of a long room*

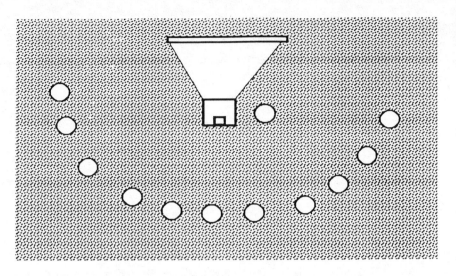

Figure 50.2   *Screen placed on the long wall of a long room*

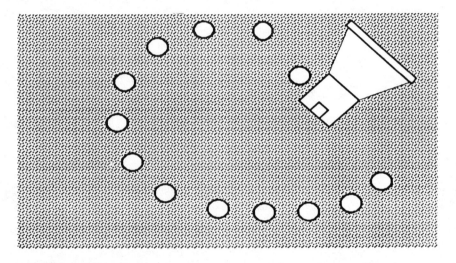

Figure 50.3   *Screen placed in the corner of a room*

If you place the screen on the short wall of a long room, quite a few participants are looking sideways at the screen (Fig. 50.1); whereas placing the screen on the long wall enables more participants to see it at a comfortable angle (Fig. 50.2).

It can sometimes be comfortable to project in a corner (Fig. 50.3). The walls may help your voice to carry better (especially if you are competing with outside noise). Also, corners are often relatively dark, so the image may show up better.

The mechanics of the thing!

There seem to be as many types of overhead projector as there are workshop venues. The less time you have to spare, the more likely you will find one of those machines which comes in a self-contained box, unassembled, and without any instructions. Get there early, play with it till you know all its foibles. Whenever possible, have a spare projector around the corner.

Colourful OHPs

Even when preparing acetates with a desk-top publishing set-up, you can bring in some colour by using coloured sheets of acetate. This can bring variety and professionalism to a presentation. If you are very fortunate, of course, you may be able to produce acetates with print in various colours—though most of us have to go back to hand writing them to achieve this. Remember that not all colours are equally visible from a distance. Throw away orange and yellow pens! Even red is not easily seen from a long distance. Blue, black, green, brown and purple are safest—and an overhead transparency can be made to look more interesting by using most of these colours in it.

Designing acetates

The most common fault is to put too much information on an acetate sheet. When you are pre-preparing overhead transparencies for a workshop, you can plan to make each 'screenful' look good—and ensure that the size of the lettering is such that it will be possible to read it from the back of the room (Fig. 50.4). Using an 'unfussy' print font (or style of hand-lettering) can make a lot of difference.

Ten tips regarding OHPs

1 A visual message is very powerful—it can send a complete message much more quickly than a spoken one can be sent. It has an integral style, can elicit an emotional response like shock or pleasure, it can be attractive, lively, interesting, colourful, mood-changing, etc.
2 Keep your transparencies in order and numbered—they are prone to flying away, sticking together or making themselves invisible. Keep plain sheets of paper between them.
3 Beware of putting frames on your transparent sheets because the frames are a nuisance if they don't fit on the projector top—and there seem to be dozens of different types of projector.
4 Put up a transparency and focus it before anyone else is in the room. Walk round and check how it looks from the seats you have set out.
5 Position each transparency with the projector light off unless you are changing them very often. Your audience will get seasick and disorientated if you flap the transparencies around with the projector light on.
6 Sometimes it is helpful to use a sheet of paper to obscure most of the transparency and gradually reveal it as you talk about each point. If you have a list of checkpoints and you want to discuss each point

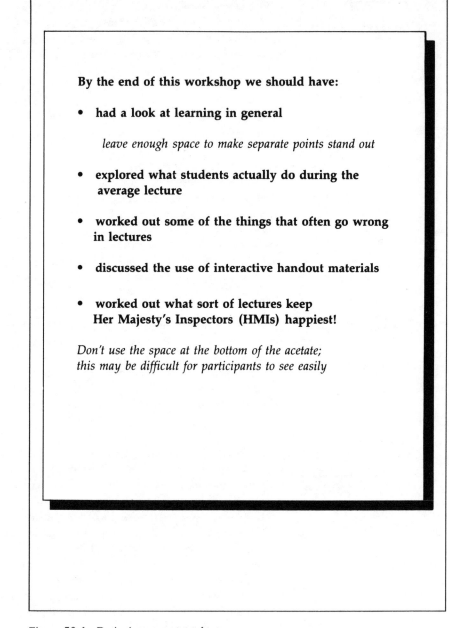

By the end of this workshop we should have:

- **had a look at learning in general**

  leave enough space to make separate points stand out

- **explored what students actually do during the average lecture**

- **worked out some of the things that often go wrong in lectures**

- **discussed the use of interactive handout materials**

- **worked out what sort of lectures keep Her Majesty's Inspectors (HMIs) happiest!**

Don't use the space at the bottom of the acetate; this may be difficult for participants to see easily

Figure 50.4   *Designing an acetate sheet*

in turn, cover the others until you get to them. Show the written point as you are talking about it, so your message is consistent and clear.

7 If you are using a blank transparency to record the main points of a discussion, make sure that your writing is clear and straight. Be sure that it is helping and not distracting.

8 Give people time to read if you are showing them words. Make sure that your verbal message and your visual message do not contradict each other.

9 You could share the fun—your workshop participants could use the OHP too. When you use it exclusively, it is a way of controlling the proceedings. If you want to open up to participation, leave the chair next to the OHP empty and encourage everyone who wants to make a point in a discussion to move there and write up their own summary or show their own transparencies.

10 Ask yourself whether you are using the OHP just because you like it. Is it the best way of providing visual aids for your purpose? Don't forget flip charts, white and black boards, handouts, large charts and diagrams, real things, demonstrations . . . .

51 Colour coding

Uses of colours

Colours are fun. Colours are significant in different ways. Colours have psychological and physical effects on people. Colours are associated with different things. Colours have uses in workshops. Facilitators can:

- Have fun with colours—use them just for fun!
- Look out for psychological and physical effects:
  - Red is likely to speed up pulses and excite; it can raise anger.
  - Blue can be deeply calming (and send everyone to sleep).
  - Green can relax and bring a balance.
  - Yellow is for sun, sunny outlooks, happiness.
- Be aware of associations that can cause unexpected reactions:
  - Black is associated with death in Western culture.
  - White is associated with purity in Western culture but death in Asia.
  - Green is associated with environment, and growing things.
  - Red is associated with danger.
  - Blue is associated with cold, and with clarity.

With visual aids

On OHP transparencies, flipcharts, boards or handouts, consider using different colours just for variety or for a particular purpose such as distinguishing one thing from another or showing similar things in the same colour.

To emphasize writing or diagrams

You can use different colours for different parts of a diagram to clarify it; for writing about different things; or to identify different people's contributions.

To distinguish one thing from another

You can use different coloured paper for handouts on different topics; use different coloured pens for 'before' and 'after' writing or drawing—this works well with transparent overlays on the OHP; use different colours to identify different groups, perhaps on badges and lists.

Effects of colours

You can take advantage of the physical effects on people that colours have, by:

- Using a lot of strong red or yellow to excite
- Using cool blues or greens to relax

- Using coloured transparencies for photocopied OHPs to reduce glare
- Using coloured paper for some handouts to reduce fatigue in reading black on white ground all the time

After-images Be aware of 'after-images' developing in people's eyes—i.e. when you stare at a colour for a short time, your eye develops the 'opposite' colour in light in reaction to it. If you look at red your eye develops green, if you look at green your eye develops red. You are not usually aware of this but it can seriously affect what you see.

Try it out by staring at something red then look away at a plain white wall—you will see the shape in bright green. Do the same thing with a green object and you will see red. Blue will turn to orange and vice versa, yellow to purple and vice versa. If you show people green elephants they will soon see pink ones. If you wear a bright green shirt, soon those looking at you will see red shirt shapes whenever they look away. This is one way to give everyone else a headache.

52 Introducing the literature

In many subject areas there is a range of literature that would be relevant and interesting but which is not necessarily easily identified in a formal library. Here is an idea that has worked for us.

Take a box of books to the workshop, more than the number of participants. Choose them from the appropriate subject area but include some quite provocative ones, some well-known core texts and some unusual and less well-known ones. Lay them out on a table and invite workshop participants to choose a book with which they are not familiar.

Ask them to read it for about half an hour, silently, and to prepare to tell everyone else about their book in terms of if and how it might be useful or interesting. Go round the group after the half-hour giving each person three to five minutes to report back. Calculate the time this will need in advance—if the group is bigger than 12 people it will take more than an hour. You could have them report back in smaller groups, then in a brief plenary, perhaps with the 'edited highlights' from each group, or the three most highly recommended reviewed. This method works very well with people who think they are too busy to seek out and use books and is often very revealing in terms of how quickly people can learn something from a book or get a flavour of its contents. The review session can raise passionate discussion!

- A variation is to do this similarly but encourage people to change books or add another if they dislike the first one or finish it quickly.
- Another variation is to ask them to look for 'good things' and 'bad things' about the book they have chosen—this could be feasible in a shorter time, say, 15 minutes to skim the book, five minutes to decide on good and bad things, then a quick round to report back.

Varying aims
- This idea is good for introducing people to a range of books and encouraging them to skim-read them and form some opinions.
- You could use this idea when you need a change of atmosphere and when a period of silence in the workshop would be helpful.
- You can use this sort of session to help people to gain confidence in their ability to pick relevance out of dense literature, to be able to select and use books confidently.
- You could ask everyone to bring along a book they have found helpful and to introduce it to everyone else—this means missing out the reading time.

Tear up a book!

(Contributed by Liz Beaty)

Yet another way of introducing participants to relevant literature is to tear it to pieces—literally. This is a powerful way of getting syndicates working quickly.

- Get photocopies of any particularly precious materials or, if the book concerned is cheap enough, sacrifice a copy by actually breaking it up into 'chunks'. (You may not believe how liberating it is to rip up a book, after years of feeling unable to even contemplate writing notes in the margins!)
- Split the resource material among syndicates, so that each syndicate has part of the whole picture.
- Get the syndicates to further divide the material equally among members.
- Give them a fixed time for every person to read his or her pages of the material.
- In syndicates, give a short time for everyone to explain to the other members of the group the essence of what they have gleaned from the material.
- Ask each syndicate to prepare a shortlist of what the members feel are the most important findings from the material that has been read.
- Get syndicates to share the important things, e.g. by using brief posters, or an overhead projection transparency of the main findings.

Variations

- It can sometimes be useful to make copies of the contents pages of the book, and issue these to all participants first, then allowing individual participants to collect elements from the book according to their main interests. The contents page can later be used as an agenda, as the whole group is asked 'Who looked at p. 23? Was it any use?' and so on.
- Pages of the book can be spread around the room as 'exhibits', and participants (individually or in groups as they prefer) can be asked to 'browse' (or even 'graze') round the room, jotting down useful ideas (with page number for reference) for later discussion. Done this way, one torn-up book can serve a number of re-runs of the workshop (though it must be admitted that the 'best' pages tend to disappear!).

53 Agenda building

First the questions, then the answers

An alternative to conveying information by means of mini-lectures or 'lecturettes' is to have a question-and-answer session, particularly when you are keen that participants have ample opportunity to set the agenda for the information exchange. The participants ask the questions and you do your best to answer them—or to help facilitate them answering each other's questions. This ensures that you provide the participants with the information that they need and also that you don't burden them with information that they don't really want.

This approach, however, has several problems. Participants may find it difficult to interact with you in your dual roles of 'expert' and facilitator. For example, some participants are reluctant to ask you, in your expert role, questions to which they really want answers but which they feel may be 'dumb' questions. You may find it difficult to combine information-giver role with facilitator role. For instance, there might be a particular sequence in presenting material that is helpful for gaining an overall understanding but which is lost in the randomness of a question-and-answer session.

A solution to these problems is to separate out the 'question' part of the session from the 'answer' part as follows:

1 Ask the participants to spend five or ten minutes discussing with a partner what they already know about the subject and what questions they would like answered. Let them know that at the end of that time you will be collecting in the questions.
2 Explain to the participants that this session will be driven by their questions so the more questions the better. Collect in the questions that have been generated by this process in a 'round robin' way. In doing this, invite participants to offer more than one question.
3 Flipchart the questions as they are being offered.
4 Answer the questions in whatever order seems to be most appropriate. You will probably want to encourage supplementary questions during this phase.

This process is rather like brainstorming where the generation of ideas is separated from the evaluation of the ideas. In this case the generation of the questions is separated from the answering part. Your roles are clarified: in the first stage you are facilitator and in the second you act as expert. Another advantage that it shares with brainstorming is that ownership of the idea/question gets lost. This is helpful to those who are fearful that their question is a 'dumb' one.

Giving the participants five or ten minutes at the start with a partner provides them with an opportunity to check out their current knowledge and to 'practise' questions in the relative privacy of a pair.

An advantage of this approach is that it sets a clear agenda for the session so you can ensure that most time is spent on those issues that seem to generate most energy in the room.

When it comes to answering the questions, you may want to group the questions on certain themes, you may want to deal with several of the questions at the same time and you may want to throw some of the questions back to the audience, er . . . participants (interesting slip there!). You may even want to throw most of the questions back to the participants. And you may, of course, simply not want to answer some of the questions at that stage in the workshop—you could, for example, use some of the questions to drive other workshop activities where the participants play a more active role than in a question-and-answer session.

Variations Instead of flipcharting the questions you can ask the participants to write their questions on strips of acetate and then these can be arranged on an overhead projector. This saves time in writing up questions on flipcharts and provides more anonymity but it doesn't give a flipchart to display on the wall as a record of where you have been. However, the acetate strips themselves can quickly be pasted (lightly) onto a flipchart, so they are still 'visible' during coffee breaks—and can be detached and re-displayed if the need should arise.

A reminder about ownership

In many parts of this book we have stressed the value of giving your workshop participants a feeling of ownership of the processes used during the workshop—and this applies just as much to setting the agenda (or re-setting the agenda as the workshop develops and unfolds). The more ownership your participants feel concerning the workshop agenda, the more they will work hard in relevant tasks and activities, and the more they will value your suggestions, and the outcomes of their own work.

54 Home groups

Participants are placed in a group called their home group, of which they remain a member for the whole workshop or for a series of workshops. It is useful to have home groups if the workshop is long or part of a series, because being in a familiar group helps participants to feel secure. This can reduce drop-outs or people falling behind, as home-group support can be substantial.

Once groups have been formed (four to nine people in a group works well) it is worth facilitating some team-building activities to allow the participants to get to know each other and plan how their group works. Some tasks for understanding and reflecting on the process of forming, storming, norming and performing will help these groups to work effectively.

Tasks for this may be short, pressured with deadlines, requiring different sorts of skills and interaction. They often involve building something, solving a problem or competing with other groups. Examples of suitable activities can be found in books of team-building tasks (e.g. Woodcock, 1989).

Once home groups are able to work together and reflect on their processes, it is possible to allocate participants to different groups for other activities and to return them to the home groups for more detailed reflection and analysis of what has been learnt. This is a very enabling process, allowing participants to consciously build up their own learning.

Once the home groups are working confidently and effectively, there are opportunities for personal objectives to be set and to be reached with the whole home group supporting each of its members.

55 Syndicate groups

Syndicate groups are subgroups of participants who go off to work on some particular task or tasks (which may be simply to discuss an issue and reach some conclusions). This is usually followed by a report-back by each group to the other participants and a plenary.

As with most group discussion methods, syndicate groups are commonly regarded as better than lectures when it comes to changing attitudes and developing commitment.

Groups of about four to eight work best as syndicate groups. As facilitator you may have reasons for wanting to determine the composition of the groups taking into account such factors as age, gender, experience and so on. Alternatively, you can simply ask the participants to form self-selected groups. The danger with the latter is that people will usually group with those people that they already know best whereas they probably have most to learn from those that they know least well.

A simple solution is to number off the participants according to the appropriate number of groups. If three groups are needed then number off (or better, ask the participants to number themselves off) around the room '1', '2', '3', '1', '2', '3' and so on until all participants have a number. Then all the '1's form a group, all the '2's form a group and all the '3's form a group.

When syndicate groups don't work well the reason is usually that they have not been given clear instructions about what they are expected to achieve and/or they are uncertain about the time limit they have for the activity.

It is usually best to give different syndicate groups different tasks. Otherwise the report-backs can become pretty boring to the rest of the participants after the first two groups have reported!

Open-ended questions make good syndicate group tasks. For example:

- What are the qualities needed by a good supervisor?
- How many ways can you think of for coping with examination nerves?
- What are the differences between supervising a full-time research student and supervising a part-time research student?

Sharing experience can also work well:

- Tell each other about an effective teacher that you have had and identify the qualities in them that made them so.

Report-backs that are entirely spoken tend to be less interesting than those that have some visual support. For this reason you might want to give each syndicate group a sheet (or sheets) of flipchart paper on which to record their conclusions.

Comments   Not everyone likes syndicate groups. They have been described as an 'organized exchange of ignorance'. This suggests a significant pitfall to avoid: it is important for successful syndicate groups that the participants have some knowledge of the issues that they have been asked to work on. This knowledge may, of course, be based not only on instruction but on experience acquired before or during the workshop.

Variations   A couple of other ways of forming 'random' groups are:

- If there are different tasks for different groups then put up a poster with spaces for people to sign underneath. The number of spaces will determine the group size for each task.
- Use a pack of cards (or a set of index cards) with colour codes—the groups are made up of all those with the same colour. Of course, if you want four groups then you can use the suits on playing cards as the criterion for group formation.

Report-backs from syndicate groups can be of variable quality. The problem is not usually in the quality of the content but in the level of interest engendered by the presentation. A device that we have sometimes used is to ask the groups to make 'symbolic presentations' such that they can only draw symbols to represent their conclusions (i.e. words are not allowed on their flipcharts). This almost always injects humour into the presentations and rarely drives out the serious points that the groups wish to make.

56 Ringing the changes

It is often best to reshuffle syndicate composition several times during a workshop. This allows all participants to interact with each other at some time during the workshop, and also can help to avoid particular syndicate groups going 'stale' (e.g. due to the presence of a particularly hostile or difficult participant).

When syndicate compositions are changed, it is easy for participants to get mixed up regarding which group they are supposed to be in. The way around this is to have on an overhead (or on a flipchart) a clear chart of names, tasks and syndicate groups.

This is best made at the workshop rather than in advance! (If you try to decide syndicates for workshop participants in advance, you can guarantee that Josephine will not turn up, but they will send Cynthia in her place, and Bob won't turn up at all!)

Another problem is overcome by making a master-list of names and tasks. As facilitator, if you just rely on your memory for 'who was in which syndicate last time' it is very easy to get confused, and end up putting people in syndicates you didn't intend to—e.g. working with some of the same people they have already worked with.

The first syndicate task

It is useful to make the master-list based on the order of the participants sitting around you. This is easiest when they are in a U-shape. The list then helps you to remember names when they return to their places in the plenary group. (Most participants return to the same positions after tasks—perhaps it is something to do with territorial instincts!)

For the first task, it is often valuable to make sure that each syndicate contains people who have not been sitting next to each other—and who therefore probably have not had the chance to chat and get to know each other. The example shown in Fig. 56.1 demonstrates how easy it is to arrange this with your master-list.

In this example, all the 'A's can be asked to form one group, all the 'B's form another, and so on. Remember to make it clear where each group is to go. If they are all in the same room, sticking cards to walls and doors can help. If they are in different rooms, the location can be written onto the acetate, beside the first occurrence of the letters.

Task	1
Name	
Helen	A
John B.	B
Allan	C
Pat	D
Maggy	A
Fred	B
Henry	C
John D.	D
Gerry	A
Tom	B
Phil	C
Viv	D

Figure 56.1 *Master-list for arranging participants into syndicates*

Figure 56.2 shows how this list may develop as further syndicate tasks are used, and how syndicate sizes, compositions, and 'convenorship' can be rotated. This shows successive tasks 1, 2, . . . 5 using respectively syndicate sizes of 3, 4, 4 (different 4s), 2, and 3 (different 3s). We leave it to you to work how to spread the influence of a particularly hostile or difficult participant. The 'squares' drawn around some letters can show which member of the syndicate is charged with taking a flipchart from the pad, or taking pens and acetates and so on. This speeds up the time taken for syndicates to get to work. The 'chosen' person can receive a briefing to start the syndicate on its task, but it is useful to make clear to everyone that this doesn't mean this person has to report back later.

Task	1	2	3	4	5	6
Name						
Helen	[A]	A	[A]	A	A	
John B.	[B]	B	A	[B]	B	
Allan	[C]	C	A	[C]	A	
Pat	[D]	A	A	D	[B]	
Maggy	A	[B]	B	E	[A]	
Fred	B	[C]	B	F	B	
Henry	C	[A]	B	[A]	C	
John D.	D	[B]	[B]	B	[D]	
Gerry	A	C	[C]	C	[C]	
Tom	B	A	C	[D]	D	
Phil	C	B	C	[E]	C	
Viv	D	C	C	[F]	D	

Figure 56.2 *Development of the master-list as tasks progress*

57 Theme bases

When you want to introduce participants to several different ideas or activities in small groups, a useful technique is to use theme bases. A base may be a table in the corner of a room, a group of chairs laid out ready for a discussion, perhaps a nearby room with specialized equipment, etc. The idea is that each group works for a set time at each base—so they might have 20 minutes at each of three bases in an hour. Each base has instructions and materials for a different activity.

How they can work

- Each base must be laid out in advance with all the necessary instructions and materials, and probably numbered.
- All workshop participants are allocated to a group; two to six people in each works well.
- Each group is engaged in a different activity for a set period of time at one of the bases.
- At a given signal or agreed time, all groups move on to the next base, the next activity, maybe in sequence.
- When each group has visited each base, a plenary session pools reactions to each experience.

Ways of using theme bases

In a workshop for trainers, we have used bases like this:

Base 1   Discuss ways in which a trainer can evaluate the success of a session.

Base 2   Prepare a presentation on how visual aids can be used (a variety of materials and equipment should be available).

Base 3   Watch this video and make a flipchart of the main points of interest you draw from it (the video should be left wound back and with operating instructions handy).

Base 4   Here is a list of problems a trainer might encounter. Discuss, agree and write on a flipchart the solutions your group suggests.

Base 5   (A separate room with light-weight chairs and tables.) Agree the best way to arrange this room for the training sessions described (a list is given of different topics, numbers, approaches, etc.). Make sketch drawings of your proposals.

These bases give rise to groups having things to present to everyone, so the feedback session needs to be quite long.

If the workshop had been on the use of visual aids, there could have been bases on making things, on discussing the use of different sorts of visual aid, on finding out how an OHP works, on practising the use of different sorts of equipment, etc. The plenary might be a series of short presentations after a short break in which each group prepares a presentation of its findings.

This is a good technique for enabling participants to work at their own pace in a variety of activities, but it is essential that it is really well prepared.

Preparation checklist

- Match the number of activities to the number of participants and groups planned, perhaps having an optional one you can leave out if numbers are not really known in advance.
- Make activities suitable to last the same length of time—half an hour works well with about four bases. Too many is tedious.
- Make sure instructions are clear (try them out on a critical friend) because you can't deal with four problems at once.
- Make sure you have put out all necessary materials, equipment, tables and chairs.
- Be prepared to hover helpfully.
- Each group will take different lengths of time in spite of your planning—put in optional tasks and be prepared to move some groups on fairly forcibly.
- Ever-ready coffee between bases helps oil the wheels . . .
- The plenary is fairly unpredictable—some groups like to discuss every detail of their experiences.

The compensation for so much advance preparation when using theme bases is that the facilitator has very little to do while they are running and can observe and work with participants in a very relaxed way. It can be a good idea to build in a few breaks, or let participants decide their own break times within a general structure of 'moving on' times.

It is quite possible to run a session like this with 40 participants and one facilitator—it would be an adventure to try with more—but if there are several facilitators available, this may be a good way of using particular specialisms, as bases can be separately facilitated mini-workshops. Similarly, you can have a mixture of staffed and unstaffed bases, particularly if some need skills demonstrated or technical help.

58 Using music

Music can make a workshop more productive and more enjoyable. It can add variety to a workshop. It can also serve much more specific purposes. Here is a list of when and how you might want to use music in your workshop:

At the start   When participants are registering, some suitable music can help to create the mood that you want for the workshop. It also helps to break the ice for participants who have not met before: it creates noise so that conversational gambits are less intrusive than if the room were silent and it can also serve as a topic for conversation. Furthermore, showing this level of attention at the start of a workshop (when many participants are feeling anxious about being with a group of people that they don't know) helps them to feel nurtured by the workshop facilitators.

We have often used Vivaldi's 'Four Seasons' as background music when participants are registering. In fact, we find that most of the music of Vivaldi is pretty suitable.

Pacing   Music can be used as a signal when you wish to encourage participants to restart work at the end of a break or at the end of a session of groupwork. We sometimes use some rock music for this. The track entitled 'Let's work' by Mick Jagger from his LP entitled 'Primitive Cool' has worked well for us: it has an appropriate lyric and is loud and insistent. It is a good piece for raising energy for the next part of the workshop.

Creating a new mood   Music can be very helpful in creating a mood appropriate to an activity. For example, you may want to play soft and peaceful music to accompany a visualization exercise. You may wish to use quiet music with an even tempo as an accompaniment to a reflective activity.

Accelerated learning through music   Music can stimulate creativity. The reason for this seems to be that music engages those parts of the brain that process non-verbal, holistic, spatial and emotional information— which seems to be the source of much of what we term 'inspiration'. Some people refer to this as 'right-brain thinking' as there appears to be some specialization on these skills in the right side of the brain. Moreover, music with particular rhythms can help to bring about a state of calm and relaxed alertness. This state is associated with so-called alpha and theta brainwaves which are conducive to effective learning. The rhythms of Baroque music seem to be particularly well suited to this state. So you may want to include in your repertoire of workshop music some of the works of Bach, Corelli, Handel, Telemann and Vivaldi.

59 Feeling your way

Workshop participants are people (so are facilitators). Two things are certain: people have feelings about the way a workshop proceeds, and different people feel differently about the same workshop. The more you know about the feelings at your workshop, the more you can tune in to them.

Take time to look

You can tell a lot about how your participants are feeling by taking time to observe them. Some signs of unproductive feelings include:

- Participants who sit with arms folded in front of them. They are usually feeling turned off—perhaps because they know all about what is going on.
- Eyelids half-closing—this probably means you are talking too much, and participants are not getting the chance to contribute as they wish.
- A few participants who always seem to be making quiet asides to each other—this probably means there is another agenda that you don't yet know about.
- Pained expressions on the faces of some participants every time some other participant speaks—it is quite common for participants to generate tensions in each other.

Bring out the feelings

One of the most productive ways to acknowledge that people have a right to have feelings is to bring their feelings out into the open. Here are a few quick ways of doing this.

Ask the question

Ask each participant to reply to the question 'How do you feel?' in just one or two well-chosen words (put the question on a flipchart or overhead, and transcribe their responses onto a flipchart). This allows participants to reply directly. You will get all sorts of replies including:

- stimulated
- confused
- all right
- hungry
- challenged
- tired
- bored
- annoyed
- happy

and so on. After having collected the range of feelings, you can decide whether or not to probe deeper into the reasons for particular feelings such as 'confused' or 'annoyed'.

Jotted notes

Ask participants to jot down a few words about how they feel using Post-it slips or small squares of acetate. This allows participants the comfort of anonymity if they wish to raise particular issues. The Post-its can be placed on a flipchart, or the acetate squares can be shown on the projector a few at a time, then attached to a flipchart. Participants feel better when their feelings are displayed for future reference—they see that you are trying to take their feelings into account as the workshop develops.

Mini-questionnaires

You can have a stock of small (less than A5) slips of paper which already have various feelings words or statements printed on them (Fig. 59.1). Give these out and ask participants to ring or underline words or phrases that apply to them. This has the advantage that you can help participants bring into the open various feelings they may have been reluctant to express if the words were left to them. However, make sure that you leave a little space for 'other feelings . . . ' so that participants who have feelings you have not covered can express them.

How is the workshop going for you?

Circle the words that apply

fine	*all right*	*too slowly*
stimulating	*too quickly*	*challenging*
boringly	*useful*	*not addressing*
know most already	*great*	*my problem*

Other comments:

Figure 59.1 *A mini-questionnaire for gathering feelings*

Happy faces

Either on Post-it slips, tiny bits of acetate, or by using a flipchart, ask the participants to draw a 'face'—smiling, frowning, puzzled, and so on (Fig. 59.2). This method can be less threatening to participants, who, for example, can draw an 'unhappy' face without having to explain to you exactly why.

Someone else's feelings

Ask each participant to talk for a minute to one or two colleagues, then report back giving someone else's feelings (but without naming the someone else), along the lines 'One of my colleagues feels . . . ' This

Figure 59.2   Drawing faces as a means of expression

method helps bring participants closer together by sharing their feelings with each other, and representing each other in the report-back of feelings.

Your feelings   Your feelings can be hurt! You may want to share your feelings too—or you may want to hide them. We leave this to you to decide!

60 Mid-workshop feedback

Despite the virtues of employing questionnaires at the end of workshops to gain feedback from participants, they are usually employed too late to do anything about things that are wrong, and questionnaires by their nature have limitations on the breadth of feedback they can engender. It is possible simply to ask participants 'how is it going?'—but this does not always get you the feedback you really need; people tend to be too polite! The following idea will get you rapid feedback during a workshop, so that you will be able to put it to immediate use.

Obtaining feedback

A quick and penetrating way of getting feedback during an event is as follows.

- Give each participant a Post-it slip.
- Ask them to write the words stop, start and continue as shown in Fig. 60.1.

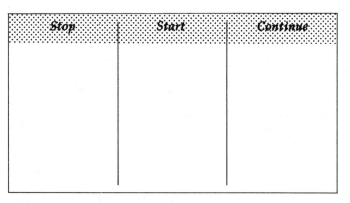

Figure 60.1   *Quick mid-event feedback on Post-it notes*

- Ask them to write what they would like you to *stop* doing, *start* doing and *continue* doing.
  or
- Ask them to write what *they* would like to stop doing, start doing, and continue doing.
  or both!
- Ask participants to tear their Post-it slips into three bits, and stick the various bits on flipcharts (or walls). It is useful to have three separate areas for the 'stops', 'starts', and 'continues'.

Responding to feedback

- Take particular notice of the 'stops'. You will often be told things that you did not know you were doing. You will certainly be told things that people would not have told you unless you asked them to be so specific as to tell you what to stop. Of course, don't panic as soon as you see all the things you may consider stopping—other participants will often have mentioned exactly the same things under 'continue'.
- It is often useful to discuss the 'starts' briefly with the group. It can be productive to put the main items from the 'starts' onto a flipchart, and ask the group to prioritize them. The 'starts' provide a quick way of finding out about 'matters arising'—and a good way in that everyone has an equal 'say' (unlike oral mid-workshop feedback, which tends to be given by a minority of vociferous participants!).
- The 'continues' are your good news! Accept them and try to keep doing whatever they are. Long-term building on the 'continues' is a valuable way of developing your range of workshop skills.

Example

Here is an example of this sort of intermediate feedback, gathered during a workshop on teaching large groups, in just five minutes or less. As well as being able to fine-tune the workshop to take into account the feedback, a transcript was circulated to all participants as part of a collection of 'workshop products'.

Stop
- generalizing
- giving generalized rather esoteric theories on teaching
- using so many overhead transparencies
- dismissing educational theories

Start
- practical 'real' examples of interactive handouts which have been used
- saying what problems have been encountered when first introducing interactive handouts
- giving a clearer structure, more practical ideas to use
- succinct practical advice on communicating effectively with large groups and conveying volume information in short time
- to demonstrate how an interactive lecture would feel to a student
- to reconcile the approach with reading dynamics
- summarizing 'do's and 'don't's
- being specific, relating more to the large groups' problems
- discussing practical problems of time and facilities for preparing such teaching sessions
- relating to issues identified at the beginning
- being specific to our subjects; detail a lecture on a topic using interactive methods

Continue
- identifying key questions
- giving ideas on techniques
- explaining techniques which may be useful
- illustrating new approaches and new ideas
- discussing techniques which can be used in particular cases

- lecturing style, similar pace
- use of projector
- participation of group
- advice on personal learning techniques

61 Plenary discussion questions

Objective   • To identify a range of general questions that stimulate group reflection following a workshop activity.

The discussion at the end of a workshop activity is normally an important part of the activity. This is the reflection stage where much of the learning takes place. It provides an opportunity for discovery, swapping ideas and responses and increased self-awareness. Sometimes facilitating this discussion will not involve asking questions. For example, if there is a productive spontaneous discussion then simply keeping quiet can be the best form of facilitation. At other times reflecting back the feelings and thoughts of the participants will be helpful to their learning. There will be other times when you want to ask questions to develop a useful discussion.

Most experiential workshop activities can lead to learning at the following levels:

• perceptions
• feelings
• thoughts
• behaviour

You may want to explicitly facilitate the discussion through those four levels. Here are some general all-purpose questions which are useful for a wide range of workshop activities:

Perceptions   • What happened? (Ask participants to describe their own and others' actions during the experience. This is a non-threatening place to start. It is especially important to do this when the activity took place in groups. In this case participants are naturally likely to be curious about what went on in other groups. Helping them to get that knowledge reduces uncertainty which in turn sustains the safety of the workshop).
• What was the best thing about that?
• What was the worst thing about that for you?

Feelings   • How did you feel?
• And what other feelings did that produce?
• How do you feel about that now?

Thoughts
- What does it mean?
- What have you learned from what you have just done?
- What insights did you get from that?
- Were there any surprises in that for you?
- What is the significance of that?

Behaviour
- What are you going to do as a result of that?
- What are you going to do differently as a result of what you have learned from that exercise?
- How can you apply what you have just learned?
- What are the risks involved in acting on your insights?
- How can you use that to your advantage?
- What other options did you have in that situation?
- What other options do you have when you next find yourself in that situation?

Comments
You can think of these stages as a 'default checklist'. In practice the sequence may be very different. If the debriefing starts with participants wanting to discuss issues other than describing the experience itself then it is best to go with the flow.

The stages outlined above (perceptions ⇒ feelings ⇒ thoughts ⇒ behaviour) can also be used as the basis of a 'pyramiding' activity along the following lines:

- In pairs (from different groups if it was a group activity) compare your perceptions of what actually happened in the activity.
- Each pair join with another pair (to form a group of four) and discuss what you felt and what you learned from what you have just done.
- Each group of four join with another group of four and discuss what you might do differently as a result of what you have just done.
- Finally, hold a short plenary discussion of what has emerged from this process.

62 Dealing with difficult participants

There is always one! Well, there is often one—the participant who tends to disrupt your hard-thought plans and intentions.

Objectives
- To minimize disruption to other participants.
- To safeguard your own temper and sanity!

There is no single sure-fire way to deal with a difficult participant. After all, 'difficult' comes in all shapes and sizes, and there is just a chance that the participant is right all along. None the less, here are some options:

Analyse (privately) the problem Whose problem is it? Is it the participant's problem—and in this case is it obvious to everyone that this is so? Is it your problem? Is the real problem that you don't want to be deflected from your plans? Have you a solid reason for not being deflected—may it be worth 'giving in' and hopefully placating the participant concerned? Is it that the participant already knows more than you (or anyone else present) about the topic? (Yes, this does happen.) Dare you admit this to everyone? If not, whose problem is it?

Go right up to the participant It is easier to be disruptive if you are sitting a long way from the facilitator. If the facilitator walks right up to you and speaks quietly and purposefully to you (with everyone else wondering what is going to happen next) it is not comfortable! Few participants will risk this happening again. The actual verbal exchange can be quite simple—e.g. 'Would you like to explain to the group exactly what reservations you have—and can I write them onto a flipchart so that we can continue to keep them in mind as the workshop progresses?'

Isolate the participant—take a vote It is safe to take a vote when you sense almost everyone else is on your side. Make it a clear choice—'How many of you would like to depart from our programme and follow up the issue Fred has just raised?'

Wait till coffee time This is much kinder. Collar the participant concerned quietly (not literally) and say something similar to 'I feel that the workshop is not going along the lines that you think best. Can you explain to me exactly what we could do to make it better?' If possible, do something with the suggestions you receive—or compensate by discussing the issues there and then with the participant.

Let the rest gang up   One colleague we know has this knack. After a while, some other participant will turn on the offending one and say words as forthright as 'Fred, why don't you just shut up?' This sort of event has the advantage that immediately thereafter you have got enhanced attention from everyone present—so be ready to use it. Don't refer to Fred's plight, though, just continue.

Go into syndicates   Putting participants into syndicates means that the difficult participant can for a while influence only a few people. Meanwhile, you can go round visiting the other syndicates, being particularly helpful and winning their confidence. You could even visit the syndicate containing the difficult participant, and attempt to sort things out in that less public arena.

Re-group the syndicates regularly   This is damage limitation. When you know there is a difficult participant, make sure he or she is in a different syndicate for each workshop activity. This allows more opportunity for more people NOT to be exposed to the negative participant (someone whose views differ from yours is, of course, 'negative').

Welcome all interruptions   This you can do when you have had enough practice to be confident enough to be willing to divert from the intended programme, perhaps radically. The main thing is to get the new idea up on the wall somewhere—on a flipchart or chalkboard. Once it is there, the difficult participant will often relax. The issue need not then be dealt with straightaway, but can be left till later (or till time has run out anyway!)

Turn the interruptions into an advantage   Quite often, there is something really useful to be derived from a difficult participant. Carefully establish exactly what the complaint or view is, then put it to everyone (in groups if possible) to address for a given time. Once everyone has the feeling that the issue has been addressed, the participant will be unlikely to cause further difficulties over that issue—or perhaps any other issues. Let us be honest—it is often the unexpected questions and views that turn out to be the most useful aspects of a well-run workshop.

Preserving the peace

What do you do when participants fight? We take many different views in different situations; here are some:

- Do nothing, recognize when it is not your problem and trust them to have the social skills to cope in a civilized way.
- Encourage conflict, openly examine differences.
- Separate them, put them in different groups.
- Send them away to sort it out privately.
- Acknowledge differences, discuss ways of living with them.
- Take each aside and have a little chat!

- Use the group—'How can we help them to deal with this . . . '
- Revisit the ground-rules and discuss whether they need changes or additions.
- Revisit the objectives and discuss whether the conflict is inhibiting the group and may prevent achievement.
- Give a short talk on how learning can involve conflict and discuss how to handle it.
- Give a short talk on the creative role of conflict, and introduce a problem-solving model to look for a win–win solution.
- Remind everyone about the forming, storming, norming and performing stages of group behaviour and discuss how norms are reached.
- Smile. Ask the disgruntled participants to continue to disagree if they must, but to smile at each other while they do so.
- If you are really desperate try bribery, collusion, threats, punishment, expulsion . . . .

63 Task briefings

The heart of a good workshop is the interaction of the participants. It helps if participants are doing exactly what you want them to do—but this is not as easy to achieve as you may think. Especially when you ask participants to split up into groups, and move to other rooms to undertake specific tasks, it is all too easy for the task they actually attempt to be somewhat removed from your intentions.

Types of briefings

Spoken briefings

These are the most troublesome. Even when you think you have made the task abundantly clear, participants may come back with something entirely different from what you wanted them to do. Of course, sometimes useful things emerge from this, but in general participants become discouraged if they feel they have not been doing what was expected of them.

The longer the spoken briefing, the more likely it is that participants will just remember parts of it. We don't know who first said:

> I know you believe
> you understand
> what you think
> I said,
> but I'm not sure
> you realize
> that what you heard
> is not what I meant!

—but it was worth saying!

Overhead or flipchart briefings

These are better, as everyone can see exactly what the tasks are. However, if participants need to go to another venue to perform their tasks, it is possible for their perception of the nature of the task to change somewhat between rooms.

Printed briefings

These solve many of the problems. Participants can take their briefings with them, and all participants have exactly the information you wish them to have. Printed briefings are particularly useful when you want different syndicates to do different tasks—but each group to know what the others are doing.

Getting the wording right

Suppose, for example, you wished participants to divide into syndicates, and explore some open learning materials, looking for criteria for good materials. If the task is phrased loosely, you are more likely to be given a general discussion of strengths and weaknesses of the materials they explore, than to get what you are really after—a list of quality criteria.

Excellent lists of criteria are produced when participants are given a printed briefing along the following lines:

1 Working by yourself, explore at least three different open learning packages, for about five minutes each.

As you explore, make two lists: 'good things' and 'bad things' about the respective materials.

2 In your syndicate group, turn the 'good things' and 'bad things' into a checklist (on an acetate sheet) of short, sharp criteria for good materials, along the following lines:

Good open learning materials will:

- have plenty of . . .
- be . . . in tone and style
- avoid the learner feeling . . .
- use a layout that is . . .

Try to generate 30 criteria in your syndicate.

3 Spend the final five minutes putting the most important of your criteria in order of importance. (Write '1' beside your most important one, '2' alongside your second most important one, and so on.)

When several syndicates have all addressed the same well-structured task, it is much easier to compare and contrast the findings of each syndicate.

Timekeeping

When participants get going on syndicate tasks, time flies! It is easy for them to get into all sorts of interesting discussions—which can become their excuses for not finishing the task. There is nothing worse than two prompt syndicates having to wait for a third syndicate who have let time slip.

When the tasks are broken down into stages (e.g. A, B, C) you can tour the syndicate rooms at suitable times saying 'Please move on to task B in a minute or so', and eventually 'Another two minutes to finish task C, then please come back to the plenary room'.

Using task sheets

Often, you may want to exercise some control over the level of detail participants go into during tasks. An obvious way is to set them a limit of some sort such as:

- List five advantages
- Think of 30 criteria

A way of being rather less dogmatic is to issue a task sheet, which has just the right amount of space for the sort of answer you are seeking from participants. The instructions can be printed on the task sheet, with appropriately sized boxes for them to enter thoughts and conclusions.

64 Getting participants back

Slippage of time is an enemy of workshop facilitators. Participants who see a workshop getting progressively behind schedule soon lose trust in the credibility of the facilitator—and maybe in the credibility of the whole workshop. Here are some ways to ensure that minimal time is wasted during a workshop.

Participants need to be brought back quite often, e.g.:

- after coffee breaks
- after meal breaks
- after syndicate exercises

Coffee breaks

Particularly when participants go to another venue for coffee, there is the danger that the break will overrun. It is better to plan (and insist) on a 30-minute coffee break than to plan on (but fail to achieve) a 15-minute one. Even when refreshments are brought to the workshop room itself, breaks are still in danger of extending themselves. Some ways of making sure that participants get back on time include:

- Don't say 'Let's take a 30-minute break now', say 'Let's break now and resume at so-and-so'.
- Don't say 'Let's resume at quarter-past'—say 11.13 for example. An 'odd' time stays in participants' minds more firmly than a rounded-off time.
- Hearing may not be enough; use the overhead projector or a flipchart to let participants SEE the time for resuming. 'Please resume at 11.13' is enough.
- Having said '11.13', make sure you are there and ready to go at this time—and politely start even if people are still drifting back. You can always start with something relatively trivial, but people coming in soon get the message to be back promptly next time.

Meal breaks

It is wise to overestimate meal breaks rather than rush them. Workshops at hotels are often catered for quite luxuriously—but it always seems to take at least 20 minutes for that final cup of tea or coffee after the meal. (Also, the bar may be open!) If you ever run a workshop at an establishment that has a training restaurant, the catering may be quite splendid—but not fast!

When refreshments are served buffet-style in the workshop room, take the seemingly unprecedented step of moving the food table out so that people can get at both sides of it! It is surprising how long people will otherwise wait patiently (and unproductively) in queues. With a buffet on-site, however, there is also the possibility of everyone finishing their meal early and feeling left at a loose end—this is best avoided by planning a working lunch as explained below.

Plan a working lunch

One of the safest ways of making sure that meal breaks run to time *and* that participants are not left with a feeling of having wasted time is to plan some WORK for the meal break. There are particular types of task that lend themselves to this usage, including tasks which don't require a specified amount of time. For example:

- Exploring some resource materials or an exhibition
- Skimming through some handout material
- Writing a list of questions
- Preparing an individual exercise (on acetate, paper or Post-it) for a report-back session scheduled to commence immediately after the break (e.g. at 13.44!)

It is best if the task is definite enough so that participants are in no doubt what they need to have done before 13.44, even though they are free to do the work at their own pace and in their own style.

Syndicate exercises

Getting participants back after syndicate exercises (particularly when syndicates are dispersed in various rooms) is probably the trickiest case. If they were late back from meal breaks, it may not have been their fault—i.e. they could transfer the blame. With syndicate tasks of course it *is* their fault—but they invent tremendous reasons such as 'We'd really just got into it', 'The discussion was so interesting we didn't realize the time had flown' and so on. Ways of increasing the probability that participants will resume on time include:

- Giving a definite 'odd' time as before, e.g. 'Please return to report back at 10.21' and displaying that time on a flipchart or overhead projector.
- Asking each syndicate to appoint a chairperson, a scribe, and a timekeeper.
- Touring syndicates saying (to their annoyance!) 'Seven minutes till report-back time now please', then 'Two minutes to go, please begin to make your way back'.
- Rewarding punctuality as syndicates return. This can simply be 'Thanks for keeping so well to time' to the early returners. Or if the syndicate tasks are displayed on a flipchart (as they often will be when you have given different syndicates different tasks) writing up the actual return-times (without comment) as syndicate members return. This is particularly effective—syndicates will be very prompt next time round!

65 Role-playing viewpoints

Role play can be used in many different ways for different purposes. Its success depends on participants playing their roles reasonably comfortably, so it might be necessary to do some simple versions first to let everyone get the hang of it. Try this meeting format:

'Viewpoints' meeting

Explore how people take particular viewpoints. Outline a situation and state that a meeting is to be held to discuss what can be done to improve matters. If a topic is chosen on which everyone is likely to have different views and solutions they could play themselves rather than adopt roles, but alert them to being conscious of the processes by which people state and change their viewpoints. This can help to prepare the ground for them to adopt roles and possibly unfamiliar viewpoints.

Suitable topics may be found in the common experience of groups from similar backgrounds or subject areas, or things of common concern like how children can best be educated or disciplined, what is a healthy diet, should pets be controlled, etc. This is a very useful exercise if groups need to listen to each other more or to be better able to participate in, or work with, groups with conflicting points of view.

If participants are fairly confident about taking a role, set a meeting topic and give each participant a role and a brief about their main standpoint and any relevant minor concerns. This brief should be kept confidential and the meeting runs with each person in role, putting the point of view of their character and trying to reach a satisfactory solution for them. Good topics for this are things that need to be decided when various choices are possible, and it can be helpful to adopt fairly formal committee meeting or negotiating structures. It is often necessary to give general information about the topic to everyone as well as their own particular role in the context.

Sample situation

The meeting is of managers of shops in a pedestrianized street, planning what to do cooperatively at Christmas. There is no formal traders' association, and this is the first time you have all met together. You will need to sort out who will take the chair and if notes and action points will be taken.

Role briefs   (To give on separate slips of paper to each individual.)

1 You are the manager of a fairly large general stationery store. You have a good business in Christmas cards, wrapping paper and gifts now, and you think it would be enhanced by having a good atmosphere in the street. You have planned the decorations for your store and used up your budget—but you might be persuaded to contribute a little to joint street decorations.

2 You are the assistant manager of the shoe shop. Your main business at the moment is slippers for presents and party shoes—but you expect to do well immediately after Christmas when you have your main sale. Your manager has sent you reluctantly to the meeting, because she had been pressed to send a representative. You are quite keen to design street decorations, invite groups of carol singers and all sorts of things, but you have been told that your shop has no money to contribute. You have also been told not to agree to any longer opening hours or to attend any more meetings in work time.

3 You are the owner/manager of a general stores selling groceries and greengroceries and a range of general household goods—practically every-thing anyone would want who lives in all the terraces and flats in the area. You already open very long hours—8am to 9pm, and you don't usually do anything different at Christmas except put up a few decorations. You don't think it is worth making a fuss, are too tired to be bothered, but don't want to be disadvantaged by what everyone else does.

4 You are the manager of a children's toy shop. You want to do anything you can to draw in customers—it is the best trading time for you. You want the street to have special late night shopping events, attractions, maybe children's play groups so the parents can shop on their own for a few minutes. You have contacted a voluntary group who will run some events if the shops stay open and agree to some extra stalls in the street—they have suggested a 'Victorian Christmas' theme and would get lots of local youth groups to do things in Victorian dress. You think everyone should contribute to putting up street decorations. You have invited a representative from the local council to try to gain support. You know that the neighbouring council provides lights and installs them for similar streets in their area.

5 You are an officer from the local council who has been sent to the meeting. Your brief is to sound interested and supportive but not to agree to do any-thing. Your boss has not had time to find out what role the council might take, and wants to hear what went on at the meeting before he works it out. Your general instructions are to keep your head down and to make sure you don't involve the council.

6 You have just been elected local councillor for this ward and need to make your mark. You are very much in support of anything that will let you take a leading and visible role. You anticipate being able to cut ribbons at each end of the street to open the proceedings, to host lots of worthy charitable fund-raising events, to get lots of exposure in the local paper. You think you could invite the local paper to run some of their charity events here too.

You can invent lots more roles like these if you have a larger group—more shopkeepers would be appropriate or a representative from the local residents association who is keen to prevent noise and keep the rabble out. If you have a large group, 12 or more, you could have two or three meetings and all come together to compare the results each meeting arrived at.

It might be helpful to have some people to act as observers with careful guidance about how and what to observe, and what sort of feedback would be helpful.

Other meeting situations can easily be designed. Make sure your role briefs have some 'movers' and some wanting to maintain the status quo. Give some role briefs personal interests and have some 'flag wavers' of some sort!

66 Group role play

A successful group role play can be run with participants taking the role of a group of a particular nature. For example, management trainees can be successfully cast as groups of consultants with a particular brief to solve a particular problem. Information available to them can be dependent on resources, but it can be as realistic as actually going out and finding a company to host a real project or can be simulated with whatever information is appropriately given. This sort of project leads to a group presentation of results, possibly using all other participants as the audience and having a full discussion afterwards of the processes and problems encountered.

Here are some ideas for varying this if you have suitable participants:

Masks   Some people adopt roles more easily if their faces are hidden or they are dressed as a different character. Masks can be used to put a different face on, or happy and sad masks to emphasize how people feel in different situations. Dressing the part can be very helpful if people are practising situations in which they will have to perform in reality—work-related interviews, training situations or presentations. In adopting characters for unfamiliar roles, hats can be helpful to give a feeling of being different.

Puppets   Another way of reducing inhibitions can be by using puppets to act out a script or situation, with participants supplying the voices. This allows the decisions to be discussed rather than the performers. This can be useful if really difficult personal issues are involved.

Telephones   Internal telephone systems can be used to role play telephone interviews, different sorts of telephone manners and the impressions created, telephone counselling, telephone sales, customer care, handling complaints, etc. This can be a good way of making use of the internal telephone system which may be available when workshops are held in hotels.

In most uses of role play it is essential to have some observers and to be prepared to intervene in providing positive feedback and in under-lining the learning points.

67 Simulations

Simulations are attempts at creating realistic situations away from where they really happen to allow people to learn without causing real damage, losses, disasters, etc.

It is often possible for simulations to provide a protected environment in which participants can act and discuss their actions. They can allow experienced practitioners to compare different ways of dealing with situations, and for people to try out new roles. This is not really about adopting different roles, so much as being yourself in different situations.

Situations need different amounts of preparation and support; e.g. it can be helpful to use real premises when they are not open for normal business—this is good for training situations, in a field like retail training. However, quite a lot is possible in ordinary workshop conditions. Here are some examples of ways we have used simulations:

Trainer training   A familiar and often used simulation is to ask trainers in training sessions to prepare and deliver a training session in their training area. The situation is very realistic for the one doing the training, for the others it is an experience of being a trainee often in an unfamiliar subject area. Once the session is completed, there is a feedback session to discuss how it went, how the trainer felt about it and how the trainees felt. Participants are rather exposed in this sort of activity, and it is helpful to make sure that ways of giving positive feedback have been discussed and understood.

Leadership   It is very realistic to give groups tasks to complete when leadership is a topic of a workshop. There are many ways this can be done, from fairly easy 'doing something by a deadline' tasks to outdoor challenges. The situation is real and everyone participates unless observers are involved. It can be useful to have observers, but they can reduce the realism of the situation. Whether observers are identified or not, the usefulness of the simulation relies heavily on the quality of feedback to the leader and the degree of reflection each group can achieve after each task.

First aid   We have experienced some frighteningly realistic simulations of accidents—lots of 'blood', chain-saws and axes, etc. Much can be done with paint, Vaseline and tissue paper . . . However, when these mock wounds are encountered in fields and woodlands the trainee first-aiders are likely to experience the emotional reactions to the 'accident' as well as to have to think up what to do. It follows that facilitators must be prepared to deal with the emotional responses as well as straight subject matter—this is always the case but perhaps more easily recognized in this setting.

Management development   There are many ways of simulating different sorts of management experience as so much of it concerns interactions with other people, and workshops have lots of people as resources. To focus on time management and organizational skills, planning, marketing, etc., many exercises can be designed in a realistic way. These can lead to groups developing and marketing new products or putting up exhibitions on particular topics, or carrying out real projects for real clients and presenting their work in reports and verbal presentations.

In building their skills in particular situations, participants in simulations are also building their skills as observers and reporters, and their ability to give useful feedback.

68 Fishbowl interviews

Role play is a good way to develop interviewing skills. Individuals can be either the interviewer or the interviewee and can adopt the role to different extents. If this is done with non-participants watching, it is like performing in a fishbowl—ignoring the outside world and concentrating on the situation in your 'bubble'. It can be very realistic if people play themselves but in a simulated situation.

For example, job interviews can be simulated with the interviewee writing a formal application for a job which has been advertised and for which they have acquired detailed information. Others in the group can prepare an interview for that particular job, drawing up an ideal candidate frame and preparing panel questions. The interview can then be held, possibly even with everyone dressing appropriately and in a specially prepared room, and either a video recording made or some workshop participants briefed to act as observers. The debriefing session following the simulated interview should concentrate on positive feedback for both interviewee and interviewers, making sure that comments relate to things that can be changed, not physical characteristics or long-held mannerisms.

Similarly, interviews can be totally role played if the purpose is to explore the process, the ways of holding an interview, rather than how individuals perform in personal terms.

However, it can be easier to feedback personal problems if they are exhibited as part of a role play than if someone is being themselves—e.g. some people are inclined to respond to questions in a defensive or aggressive way and a role play can provide a vehicle through which this could be demonstrated and discussed. Appropriate topics can include grievance interviews, disciplinary interviews, appraisal interviews, selection interviews, etc. Briefs can be very detailed and full, or each individual can decide their own material after being given the general scenario which led to the interview being held.

Fishbowl interviews can be particularly good for examining ways of handling difficult one-to-one situations, for example to explore some counselling techniques or training techniques. This sort of session needs very careful handling of feedback afterwards to protect those who played the roles and to help everyone to learn from the experience.

Example   An example of this in use is with a group of tutors in a training session, looking at the problem of how to deal with a student who smells! The tutor has been approached by several other students who have said that they can't stand it any longer, and something must be done.

It is worth giving a little time for general discussion before adopting roles. Describe the situation, and discuss possible courses of action. Then ask for volunteers for the roles, and give each a few moments to prepare their thoughts.

One person takes the tutor role and one the student role and they hold the one-to-one meeting in the centre of a circle of observers. The tutor has avoided saying anything so far, and has asked the student to stay behind for a private word. The interview begins . . .

Once some conclusion has been reached, both role players may feel quite exposed. This sort of issue deals with things which are taboo subjects for normal discussion, and they may feel that they have exposed habits or prejudices which leave them feeling uncomfortable. Give them a chance to speak first about how they felt during the interview and how they feel now. Hold a general discussion about difficulties of dealing with such emotive issues. Allow time to deal with whatever comes up. Perhaps you would prefer to try the group out on something less exposing first. This session works with a fairly sensitive group who are all able to contribute to picking up the pieces, but such a session leaves everyone with a lot to think about and, perhaps, to confront within themselves.

69 Visualization

Visualization is a technique which involves the participant in taking a journey into their imagination. It can be a very short session or quite extended, depending to some extent on how receptive the workshop participants are to the technique, how much they trust the facilitator, etc. It is important to develop a good atmosphere for visualization activities and gentle background music or a prior session on relaxation may help.

Examples

Personal image Something which has been extensively used in slimming clubs may be helpful in other areas. Participants should be asked to close their eyes and imagine themselves as they are at this moment then to imagine themselves as they would like to be—it much depends on your group and why you are using the visualization. An example is with people considering careers or changing careers, to think about how they would like to look, how they would like to behave, where they would like to be, what they would like to be surrounded by, who they would like to be with, etc. This needs to be in their daily life rather than holidays, but don't squash elements of fantasy. Participants are then asked to open eyes and make notes of what they thought of without talking to anyone. The next stage involves focusing on how they could plan to move from where they are to where they imagined themselves.

Group planning We have used visualization successfully with groups who are in a workshop together to plan something about the future. An example is a group of people who worked together in a charity that offered help to families with many different types of problems, often very urgent crises. The session was addressing time-management, particularly how individuals caused problems for each other because of the way they managed their own time. There were personal and organizational issues bubbling up and much plain speaking, so the facilitator decided to try visualization to try to focus on improvement rather than allocating blame! The group were asked to close their eyes and picture themselves at work; then to picture a 'fast film' of a perfect day in which everything ran smoothly and led to satisfactory conclusions. They were asked to open their eyes and make quick notes of the main features of their vision. The group then shared their visions and looked for ways in which they could change their organization to make the visions possible. The general ideas were pursued into detailed action plans, many of which were in fact carried out.

Role models   Participants may be asked to think of a person they admire, perhaps in their professional field. They should try to identify some of the particular features which make this person a success—groups may discuss this at this stage. Once everyone has some idea of these features, ask everyone to shut their eyes and picture themselves at work. Then remind everyone of the features discussed, asking them to imagine how they would be different if they possessed the same features. Allow thinking time but no talking or interruptions. When all features have been considered, ask the group to open eyes and silently write notes for themselves on the differences they thought of. Then ask them to try to write down how they could make themselves as they imagined—what would it take to move from this state to the imagined one. It may be possible to move then into a group discussion on things people want to raise about the possibilities, but this can touch very delicate areas very quickly, so facilitators must be prepared to protect individuals from exposure or from being pressed to reveal anything which they would prefer to keep private.

Relaxation

Use of visualization is quite common in relaxation techniques. The normal process is to do some stretching exercises then to lie down comfortably with eyes closed. The facilitator talks slowly and quietly through a sequence of deliberately relaxing each part of the body, then moves to the face, the eyes and consciousness of breathing. Then to the mind and thoughts—it is very hard to think about nothing, so suggestions are made. This can be images or sequences of images, sometimes journeys. There are cassette tapes of relaxation talks and books of scripts available. It is helpful to have been on the receiving end of a relaxation exercise to be confident of having an appropriately relaxing tone of voice, and to understand how it feels to be talked into a deep relaxation. Facilitators should be very careful of not going outside their area of experience when working with physical exercises—even gentle stretches are dangerous for some people. Similarly, if you are interested in using this approach, you should be aware that people can have bad experiences in their imagination and may need help afterwards to deal with their encounters.

Start with a relaxation. Participants should find a comfortable space to lie down, preferably on the floor with a coat over them should they feel cold. The lights should be very low. Everyone should get comfortable and close their eyes. The facilitator should play some quiet background music, something gentle—perhaps L'Apres Midi d'un Faun' by Debussy, or gentle flute music. Talk them into a relaxation using a gentle almost monotonous voice:

Make sure that you are comfortable. We will spend some time checking through our bodies to make sure we are relaxed. Take your attention to your left foot. Wriggle it a little then relax it. Be aware of your left ankle and make sure it is relaxed. Move your attention up your leg to your left knee—tighten it to feel it clearly, then relax it. Work your way up your thigh making it relaxed, then pay special attention to your hip checking how it feels when it is tight, then relaxing it.

Talk on similarly through each leg and arm, then face, neck, shoulders, chest and stomach. Finish by saying:

Be aware of your breathing, do not change it at all, but feel the air gently entering your lungs and leaving.

A visualization script that can be fairly safely used is to ask them to:

Imagine going towards a door. Look in detail at the door—is it big? What is it made of? Is it coloured? The door opens slowly. What do you see? You are welcome to go through. The door stays open behind you and you can go back at any time. Where are you? What sort of place are you in? Do you want to explore it? Perhaps there is something helpful here for you. It is safe to wander around in . . . You might meet someone who can help you or answer a question for you. Explore this world for a while, remembering that the door back is still open, and I will tell you when we are all going back in a few minutes.

After a few minutes say:

It is time to go back now. Take a last look at the world you are in and prepare to leave it. Move back towards the door and look through it to where we came from. Go through the door and close it behind you. You can go back another time if you want to. Be aware of your body now, how heavy it is feeling, how relaxed it is. Slowly start to wake yourself up—be gentle. Perhaps move a hand or foot slightly. Open your eyes when you are ready, then sit up, but not too quickly.

This script works well for people with a general range of problems to explore—but be prepared for it not to work for everyone! It is worth concluding with a comment that once a person has learned the technique of relaxing themselves like that they can do it for themselves at any time, and can also re-run the visualization whenever they like by themselves.

70 Using videos

It is increasingly common for workshop facilitators to ask for video pro-jection facilities as a routine part of their lists of requirements. However, it is only too easy to use video in ways that don't really add much to a workshop—and indeed the risk of boring participants is often underestimated.

Appropriate use

The following suggestions should help you make appropriate use of video when necessary:

- Work out exactly why you wish to use a video in your workshop. Is it just to give you a break from facilitating?
- Remember that attitudes to broadcast television are very passive. Most of us quickly forget most of what we see on television screens—how-ever good the programmes. Some people (including the writer!) are lulled to sleep very easily by television sets!
- What exactly are your participants going to gain from watching the video? Make sure there are some definite aims.
- Work out how best to let participants know what they should be trying to extract from their experience of watching the video. For example, give them a briefing paper with some questions, to which they can jot down their own answers as the video proceeds.
- Don't just show a video, then press on, ignoring what participants have just seen. Always have some sort of debriefing activity, e.g. asking for questions based on the video, or suggestions arising from ideas it has given participants.
- If the video is genuinely being used for 'fun' or light relief, say so—and preferably plan it for an appropriate slot in your workshop, e.g. the last evening slot in a residential workshop.

Practicalities

- Check that the machine is working properly (and that you know exactly how to work it) before even mentioning that you have got a video to show.
- Rewind the tape to the exact position you wish to start from (we have seen facilitators taking several minutes to find their starting point—this reduces their credibility).
- Don't play the sound too loud—people don't like being 'blared-at'.

Start with the sound fairly quiet, and ask 'Is the sound level all right for everyone?'

- Remember that natural attitudes to video are passive, and don't expect your audience to observe every nuance of what is on it.
- Remember that concentration spans are short; a few choice three-minute clips now and then usually work better than a 30-minute straight video.

71 Case studies

Once participants have some theory and techniques in a particular subject area, it is useful to try these out by using a case study. A case study usually consists of:

- A situation that either is real and has occurred or that is invented but realistic. This needs to be communicated, perhaps by a written description, a verbal presentation probably accompanied by a summary, or possibly a video. The written information can be brief or very thorough.
- A task to complete using the material and applying the skills and theories relating to the subject area.
- A timescale within which to complete the task or tasks. A case study can last for a few minutes or for a week or so, depending on the detail of the information, the degree of realism, and the number of different tasks that can be derived from it, etc.
- Instructions as to how the participants should present their conclusions.

Case studies have worked well for us when:

- Participants have enjoyed the material and had fun using it.
- Participants have been aware of using newly acquired skills and theories and have been excited by making them work or discussing their failures.
- The case studies have been realistic and addressed real concerns, have been worth spending thinking time on and have raised emotional responses.
- Facilitators have not had a predetermined 'right' solution.

72 Verbatim comments

Often it is tempting to provide a summary of discussion at the end of a debrief or plenary session following an activity. The danger with this is that you introduce your own material in the summary and the participants decide that that is the 'right answer' that they were supposed to have discovered. At subsequent plenaries they are then more inclined to keep quiet and wait for you to tell them the 'right answer' or what they were supposed to have discovered.

Alternatively, as facilitator, you can decide not to summarize at all, but this can leave the exercise 'up in the air' with no sense of conclusion. One solution to this is to make 'verbatim' notes of significant comments that occur during the discussion. At the end of the discussion you achieve closure by simply reading back the verbatim comments. This gives a sense of progress in terms of where the discussion has travelled and what has been achieved in the discussion. Also, it can be powerful to participants to hear their own comments read back to them in their own words.

This activity is easiest to implement if you have two facilitators. One can then be responsible for facilitating the discussion while the other is responsible for recording the verbatim comments.

73 Quick rounds

Quick rounds are usually organized with everyone sitting in a circle such that everyone is asked to make a contribution in sequence round the circle. Alternatively it may be opened for everyone to toss in a contribution as they feel moved to do so—this depends on your purpose and your group. Quick rounds are useful to change the mood of a workshop in a short time. We have used them at different times during a workshop:

- at the beginning of a day
- at the beginning of a new session
- to introduce a new mood or topic
- to finish off a session
- to end a phase

They have the effect of *bringing the focus back to the whole group* after individual or small group work, or after a break.

Introductions

When a new group has been formed, introductions can be handled in a quick round. It depends on your workshop how much you want people to reveal at this very early stage, but we often use the following methods:

- 'My name is Tom/Phil/Viv, please would each person tell me your name?'
- 'Please would each person tell us your name—the name you would like us to use in these sessions not your whole title' (this may be necessary if people are used to formal settings and you want to establish an informal atmosphere).
- 'Please would each person tell us your name and a little about why you have come to the workshop' (only if you already know each other a bit or you are sure that this will be answerable without embarrassment).
- 'Please would each person tell us your name and where you work, or a little about your work' (again, only with appropriate groups—the danger with this is that it can be a slow round unless the first one gives a snappy model to follow).
- 'Please tell us one thing you would like us to know about you' (if names are not needed or to focus on variety in the group).

Starting a new topic

This is one way to check out previous knowledge and experience briefly when introducing a new topic. This enables the facilitators to use the experience of the group and enables everyone else in the group to appreciate the needs and interests of each other. Useful methods are:

- 'Please say a little about any experience you already have with this topic.'
- 'Please tell us what you would like to get out of this session.'
- 'Please tell us what this topic means to you.'
- 'What do you want to find out today about this topic?'

Checking the agenda

It is useful to agree the agenda at the beginning of a workshop or maybe at the beginning of a session within a workshop. You might want to gain agreement over what the content should be, or agreement over how much time should be allocated for each item. You might want to discuss the process if the group are conscious of how they learn.

Here are a few ideas for agreeing aims and objectives for the session:

- Share plans for the session and ask each person to prioritize their personal interests, perhaps by asking 'Tell us the three things most important to you.'
- Ask 'What would you add and what would you subtract from this agenda?'
- Use a sentence completion round in which everyone adds their own ending to 'What I would like to concentrate on in this session is . . . '
- Similarly, 'What I can contribute to this session is . . . '

Checking feelings

Sometimes during a workshop, or at the beginning of a new day on extended workshops, it is useful to check how everyone is feeling. Rounds to check feelings can be a new idea for some participants, so if it is the first time you have tried it it may be helpful to give more detailed instructions, examples or to go first yourself. One possible method is sentence completion:

- 'What I like about this workshop is . . . '
- 'What I don't like about this workshop is . . . ' (this one may need careful handling and might be best used with a supportive group)
- 'What I like about this group is . . . '
- 'What I don't like about this group is . . . '
- 'What I'd like more of in this group is . . . '
- 'What I'd like less of in this group is . . . '
  or
- If people get restless or frustrated try completion of 'What I'd like to do now is . . . '

It helps to get everyone to turn their chairs round so the circle is facing outwards and no one can make eye contact. This can be developed by closing eyes and thinking for a few moments, perhaps with a question to ponder or a sentence to complete.

Endings

Rounds can be used as a way of finishing a session or workshop. Some ideas are:

- 'Please would everyone tell us one thing they have learnt today.'
- 'Please will everyone tell us one thing that they will remember from this workshop.'
- 'Please tell us one thing you intend to do as a result of this workshop.'

General points about rounds

Many of these ideas can be extended to having buzz group discussions before the round, for example, or giving time to think before saying anything. For some people it can be quite threatening to have to make a contribution in turn and they will worry about what to say rather than listen to everyone else, so it can be kinder to ask for contributions rather than to have an enforced pattern for people to speak.

Rounds can become very tedious if the group is large—the greater the numbers the more important it is to have precise questions or statements. Think hard about ways of using rounds if your participant number is more than 20.

74 Overnight work

When a workshop spans two or more days (residential or non-residential), there is often considerable value in setting participants some overnight work. There are, however, some things to take into consideration when deciding the nature and scale of overnight tasks.

How much work?

In a residential workshop, there will probably be dinner, then the temptations of the bar to contend with. In a non-residential workshop, some participants may be able to manage to find as much as six hours 'overnight'—but others will have existing commitments that will preclude them spending much time at all on work. Therefore, a sensible compromise for both kinds of workshops is that it should be possible to complete the overnight tasks in not much more than an hour. This does not prevent participants who wish to do more work from doing so.

Advertise it

When overnight work is 'sprung' on participants (especially at non-residential workshops), there can arise quite strong feelings about the imposition of such work! Participants who already have commitments can be quite vehement in their opposition to the concept of such work. If it is known in advance that there will be overnight tasks—and the approximate extent is indicated on the advance programme—overnight work is usually accepted readily.

What sort of overnight work?

It is best that a printed briefing is prepared. The problem with putting a briefing on a flipchart or overhead is that somehow it seems to 'transmute' overnight, and people return having done a variety of variations on the intended task.

The nature of overnight work should be decided with the following points in mind:

- Things that participants can do better on their own than in a room full of people.
- Things that will save time in the next stage of the workshop.
- Things that participants can do on their own, then discuss in plenary later.
- Things at which some participants may be slower than others, and can be spared the embarrassment of being seen to be slower.

Agree on a tangible outcome

Overnight work is much better accepted when it is abundantly clear exactly what is expected. There are various ways of helping everyone to perform the work to the standard that is intended, e.g.:

- Issue a checklist or pro-forma to be filled in, recording the main outcomes of the work

  or
- Agree that everyone reports back with one overhead transparency summarizing their conclusions from the overnight work

  or
- Agree that everyone prepares a flipchart to be exhibited and discussed in the next session.

Overnight work *not* to set

- Reading whole textbooks or manuals; it is far better to prescribe particular sections or pages instead.
- Anything people are likely to get stuck on; save the tasks for which support is needed until support is available.

75 Time to use handouts

The content of a good workshop is often less important than the processes participants engage in during the workshop. It can be profitable to wrap-up important elements of the content in the form of handout materials, so that minimum time is wasted getting the content across to participants (who can in any case read a lot faster than you can talk). Handouts can be issued before, during and after workshops—or any combination of these.

When to use

There are advantages and disadvantages to be weighed up regarding various ways of timing your use of handouts. There are no 'best options'—it is worth exploring the pros and cons yourself and maximizing the benefits, while minimizing the risks. We have given three advantages and three disadvantages for each of several possibilities below.

In advance

1 A complete pack of handouts issued in advance:

Advantages
- Participants can tell exactly what the workshop is going to be about.
- Participants can 'get to know you' in advance through the way you explain ideas in the handouts.
- Your workshop looks as though it has been particularly well prepared (at least in terms of the content to be covered).

Disadvantages
- If there is too much information, participants may find it threatening.
- Any participants who are last-minute substitutes are immediately disadvantaged.
- Participants who for some reason are 'hostile' to the topic of the workshop may find all sorts of things to disagree with, and come to the workshop well-rehearsed in airing their reservations.

2 Individual handouts issued in advance:

Advantages
- Participants have the opportunity to prepare for the workshop.
- It may be possible to start the workshop taking agreed knowledge for granted.
- An early workshop task can be set where participants develop ideas they have taken from the handouts.

151

Disadvantages   • Some participants will not have had time to read the handouts in advance.
  • There will always be one participant who didn't receive the handout at all (or so she will claim!).
  • Some participants may decide that since they have got the handouts, they need not turn up for the workshop.

3   Different handouts issued to different participants in advance:

Advantages   • A cunning way of planting different kinds of expertise in the group, which can lead to everyone being able to shine in one task or another at the workshop.
  • The fact that there is not too much pre-reading for any particular participant means it is more likely to be done.
  • Participants may feel reassured knowing that they have prepared themselves in particular ways ahead of other participants.

Disadvantages   • The participant who had the key paper on 'grobulism' may not turn up due to a dose of 'flu—and no one else knows a thing about 'grobulism'.
  • You may lose track of which handouts you issued to which participants—this can be embarrassing.
  • Everyone will want to 'catch up' on the various resource materials—generating some anxiety.

At the start   **Handouts issued at the start of sessions:**

Advantages   • Participants get the uplifting feeling of being empowered with information.
  • Participants are encouraged to be back promptly after breaks.
  • Everyone receives the same information at the same time, and feels equally prepared for tasks based on the handouts.

Disadvantages   • Participants may browse through the handouts instead of paying attention to the exact briefings for workshop tasks.
  • Some participants may 'switch off' mentally, believing they already possess what they came for.
  • Participants may resent having to wait for handouts until you issue them ('Why couldn't you have sent me this earlier?').

In the middle   **Handouts issued in the middle of sessions:**

Advantages   • You do not have to rummage around for a handout specially for Mr Jones who comes in late.
  • You can prepare participants for exactly what you want them to do with the handout when they get it.
  • Pausing to give out a handout can be a welcome relief for participants if you have been talking too much!

Disadvantages
- If participants have been making notes, then find it is all in the hand-out, they feel frustrated—and probably won't take notes when you may want them to.
- Participants may start an interesting discussion while you are giving out the handouts, and not wish to stop.
- It always takes longer than you intend to get copies into everyone's hands—and it is obviously unwise to start talking about the handout until everyone has one. (It is usually quicker to give them out your-self than to push piles of handouts towards the nearest participants saying 'Please take one and pass them on'!)

At the end **Handouts issued at the end of sessions:**

Advantages
- You can have second thoughts about whether or not to issue the handout—participants may have thought of better ideas than the ones in your handout!
- A handout issued at the end can give participants the feeling of rounding-off the session in a satisfying way.
- The handouts can cover additional information that you didn't want to turn into major discussions or debates.

Disadvantages
- Participants who have made copious notes may be annoyed.
- Participants may have noble intentions to read the handouts thoroughly—but file them never to be seen again!
- Some participants may feel 'Why couldn't you have given us this earlier instead of spending all this time working it out for ourselves?'

After the workshop It is rather a special case to send handouts to participants after the workshop, but surprisingly often you will think of something during your workshop about which you would like to issue a handout—but haven't got it ready (or wish to adapt it a bit first). It may well be better to give yourself time to get the handout exactly right, rather than give out one that is not really appropriate.

Advantages
- You can include comments and issues arising during the workshop itself—this gives the handout material a 'brand new' feel. You can summarize workshop feedback comments, and transcribe important products of the workshop.
- It is often useful for participants to have some cause to think back to the things they learned from the workshop—the reflection stage of the learning process.
- You can tailor what you send to particular participants to reflect individual issues they showed interest in at the workshop.

Disadvantages
- It takes strong willpower on your part to make sure that the follow-up materials are assembled and sent off within a sensible time period (e.g. between one and two weeks after the workshop).
- Participants may just file the papers (or bin them).

76 Prepared plenary sheets

This idea can be used as either an alternative to the mass plenary or as a device for supporting it. Instead of going straight from a workshop activity to a plenary involving all the other participants, you introduce an intermediate stage in which the participants engage in some individual reflection. In this stage the participants answer some prepared questions about the activity and their responses to it.

- At the end of an activity, distribute a questionnaire containing a series of open questions with space for the participants to scribble their responses.
- The questions that you ask will depend on the particular workshop activity. Figure 76.1 gives examples of the sort of questions that might be included on a prepared plenary sheet following a syndicate group task concerned with teambuilding. In this case you would probably want to include another stage where the members of each syndicate team had some time together to compare their responses to the questionnaire.
- After this stage of individual reflection (and possibly team reflection) have a brief, full plenary. Participants are likely to be very forthcoming in this as they have had a chance to work through their own responses

---

Some review questions

- Who participated most?
- Who participated least?
- Which actions helped your team to achieve its task?
- What actions hindered the team in accomplishing its task?
- What form(s) did leadership take in your team?
- What feelings did you experience as the task progressed?
- What suggestions would you make to improve team performance?
- How can you apply what you have learned from this activity?

Figure 76.1 Types of questions to include on a prepared plenary sheet

to the activity, so the plenary is likely to take the form of comparing insights.

You may decide not to include a full plenary as the participants have spent time on individual reflection. However, we advise at least a short session with all the participants if only to satisfy their curiosity about what the others made of it.

77 Learning through assessing

One of the best ways of helping participants concentrate on judging the quality of something is to get them to assess it. The 'something' can range widely—from the action plans given by syndicates after undertaking a task, to an action plan or implementation proposal.

The act of applying assessment criteria is a way of maximizing the learning that occurs in a workshop activity. This is even better when the criteria are owned by the workshop participants themselves. Below is a sequence of operations whereby a set of assessment criteria can be generated, refined, weighted, then applied by workshop participants. First, a list of the processes, then explanations of each—some can be short-circuited or missed out altogether depending how much time is available at the workshop.

Step 1	Brainstorming criteria
Step 2	Discussing and prioritizing criteria
Step 3	Clarifying criteria
Step 4	Collecting criteria
Step 5	Grouping and adjusting criteria
Step 6	Weighting the criteria
Step 7	Recording the weightings
Step 8	Working out final weightings
Step 9	Making the final criteria list
Step 10	Preparing assessment grids

We shall run through each step in turn, with some suggestions about how it may be handled. For the purpose of our discussion, we shall take the task as the formulation of an action plan for the implementation of a new development—but the nature of the task could take many different forms.

Step 1 *Brainstorming criteria*
Ask participants to individually and without discussion write down (say) five features of a good action plan.

Step 2 *Discussing and prioritizing criteria*
Divide the participants into groups of three to five. Ask each group to shortlist the (say) five most important criteria the participants have identified, and put them in rank order (most important criterion first, and so on). This can take five to ten minutes, depending on the participants and the level of the action plans being aimed at.

Step 3   *Clarifying criteria*
It is useful at this point to ask participants (still in groups) to make their criteria as tangible as possible—i.e. so that (for example) each can be met 'very well', 'well enough', 'not really well' and 'not-at-all well'. It is also useful to ask them to keep the criteria fairly short and sharp. (This should take five minutes or so).

Step 4   *Collecting criteria*
Ask each group in turn for its top criterion, writing them on a flipchart exactly as given (putting any closely linked criteria together on the flipchart). The process is repeated for the second-top criterion from each group, then the third-top (by which time most criteria will have been collected). Finally, the group as a whole is asked for any further important criteria still missing from the flipchart. (The time taken depends on the total number of participants, but for a group of 20 the criteria can be collected in 10 to 15 minutes).

Step 5   *Grouping and adjusting criteria*
With the help of participants, put the criteria into clusters or groups and weed out overlap and duplication, possibly reducing the total number of criteria on the flipchart in the process if necessary. Sometimes it can be preferable to compose a new flipchart, if the criteria on the first chart were 'untidy' due to bunching and overlapping. (Ten minutes or so is usually enough for this adjusting process).

Step 6   *Weighting the criteria*
The criteria on the flipchart are given numbers (e.g. 1 to 12), and participants are asked to privately rank them by giving each criterion a points rating. For example, 'Suppose 30 points were to be divided among these 12 criteria, give each criterion a rating from zero upwards so that your total equals 30' (if there are more than about 20 participants it is best to ask participants to work in groups for this stage).

Step 7   *Recording the weightings*
The first criterion is selected, and each participant (or group) asked to shout out the points rating given to that criterion, a series of 'scores' being written onto the flipchart beside the criterion. Similarly, all criterion weightings are recorded.

Usually, it is clear from the collective weightings:

• Which criteria are the most significant
• Which criteria represent common agreement and which represent differences of opinion
• Whether any criteria (which may have looked plausible) turn out to be rated so low as to be insignificant (and therefore can be deleted from the flipchart)

Step 8   *Working out final weightings*
This can usually be done without a calculator—but one can be used if necessary.

Step 9 *Making the final criteria list*
The criteria are written onto another flipchart, this time in the order
determined by the ratings they have attracted. This order is often quite
different from the earlier 'importance' ratings reflected on the first
flipchart—i.e. the order is now a considered one rather than a subjective
one.

Step 10 *Preparing peer assessment grids*
The final flipchart is typed up, with the ratings, and sufficient columns
for scores to be entered for each action plan alongside each of the criteria
(see Fig. 77.1). Copies are run off for each of the participants. If there is
not time to do all of this, a master flipchart will suffice. Participants then
assess the various action plans, self-assessing their own against each criterion, and peer-assessing all the remaining action plans. All assessment
scores are processed at the end for the required number-crunching to
determine average total scores (and scores against each criterion). It can
be useful to discuss how the criteria have worked. Figure 77.1 shows a
master-grid which could be used for the comparative assessment of up
to ten different 'products' or task-outcomes (A–J), using up to eight
weighted criteria.

Of course, the format can be adjusted for lesser numbers of criteria or
'outcomes' as needed. And if participants are each assessing only one
'outcome', they only need a list of the criteria, the weightings, and a single
column for the scores they award.

			A	B	C	D	E	F	G	H
	Criteria	Weight								
1										
2										
3										
4										
5										
6										
7										
8										
	Total									

Figure 77.1 *A master-grid for assessing products or task-outcomes*

78 Building assessment skills

When workshop participants are going to be assessed in some way, a good way to prepare for this is by practising assessment skills.

Assessing written work

- Give a typical assignment or topic.
- Ask groups to devise a plan for a good answer and put it on a flipchart.
- Each group presents its plan. Discuss and perhaps give time to revise plans in groups.
- Then put the plans aside and discuss how this assignment will be marked. Are there any criteria (can you assess without criteria?); are there any restrictions like format, word count, etc.?; what is the required content?; is there a requirement to do anything particular like compare and contrast, describe, discuss, etc.?
- Develop a marking frame as a whole group and agree it as a group of examiners might.
- Each group to pass their plan to another group and groups try to apply the marking frame and prepare a report.
- Groups present their reports.
- Lessons are drawn out and flipcharted.

This general format can be used in lots of different ways; e.g. you could give the material to mark instead of generating it. A group of students were given three essays (with names whited out) to be 'impression marked' in three minutes—they were asked to grade them as pass, fail or borderline. They were surprised to discover how closely their impressions matched—and became very interested in how long people actually take to mark essays!

Assessing performance

Again, this can be practised by generating the material then assessing it and comparing the assessments. There are additional problems in the quality of observation, and this may suggest a need to devise exercises on observation before trying to assess observed performance.

Some considerations are:

- You may need to build observation skills.
- You may need to develop understanding of assessment against criteria.

- Participants may need to practise giving positive, helpful feedback.
- There may be a need to consider the effects of social relationships.
- Facilitators may need to protect some individuals and watch processes and moods very carefully.
- Participants may demand a higher standard from themselves than their usual assessors do.

79 Mini-lectures or 'lecturettes'

You will notice that we have entitled this item mini-lectures or 'lecturettes' rather than 'lectures'. The reason for this is that we don't think very much of lectures as a vehicle for learning. A mini-lecture or 'lecturette' is a short lecture and we recommend that lectures be used sparingly in workshops and kept as short as possible. In fact, several other items in this book may be thought of as ways that you can avoid giving lectures in workshops.

The aim of a 'lecturette' is to convey information (and there may be better ways of conveying information than a 'lecturette'). It is of little value in developing attitudes or developing skills.

How to do it wrong!

Ten rules for how not *to do it*

1 Don't bother with an introduction that outlines the structure and main areas that you intend to cover.

2 Ensure that your lecture is not relevant to the objectives of the workshop. If, by some chance, it is relevant, do not compound your error by pointing out the relevance to the participants.

3 Ensure that it is not relevant to the situations of the participants. Again, if by some chance it is relevant, do not show how the information that is to be provided can be of benefit to the participants.

4 Under no circumstances should you create any active communication with the participants. Do not ask questions during the lecture (even rhetorical ones) and certainly ignore any questions from the participants.

5 Make sure that participants have no opportunity to talk with each other or the lecturer. Breaking the lecture up with *ad hoc* buzz groups (where participants have a chance to talk with each other about the points made in the lecture) would be a clear violation of this rule.

6 Keep your enthusiasm for the subject to yourself. This one can be difficult but is important as enthusiasm tends to be infectious. As soon as you convey your enthusiasm to your audience you run a severe risk that some of what you say will become memorable.

7 If you are nervous about drying up then write the whole lecture out and read it verbatim to the audience. This has the added bonus that you won't ever have to look at the participants. Using brief notes on cards or on an OHP acetate would clearly lose the benefit of this bonus.

8 Don't use any visual aids. Using slides, transparencies or flipcharts is redundant if you are going to say it in your lecture anyway.

9 Don't include any anecdotes or real life illustrations.

10 Don't bother to summarize the main learning points at the end of your lecture or point out the implications of the information that you have covered.

If you follow all of the ten rules listed above you will probably never have to give another lecture.

80 How not to facilitate

Most of this book consists of suggestions for things to do at workshops; here we give a few suggestions for things *not to do*!

Things NOT to do!

Fail to observe participants' body language   Yawns, drooping eyelids, folded arms, sighs—all are telling you something.

Co-facilitate with someone you have never worked with before   However expert they are in their field, they can turn a workshop into a disaster—e.g. by going on, and on, and on! Get to know people quite well before you co-facilitate with them. Having someone *assist* you is a useful prelude to healthy co-facilitation. Similarly, assist people you intend to work with, rather than joining in on an equal basis on the first occasion.

Tell participants things they could tell you   A useful rule is never tell participants things you could ask them. Only tell them things when those things cannot be drawn out of them. It is all about ownership— the more that participants feel it is their ideas that are being developed, the more enthusiastic they will be.

Gloss over unanswered questions   It is far better to post unanswered questions or issues up on the wall (e.g. on a flipchart) than to appear to be trying to 'squash' them or 'sweep them under the carpet'.

Read out to participants things they can read for themselves   It is so easily done! Reading out to participants things they can see on the screen, or on a flipchart, *annoys them*! Similarly, reading out extracts from handouts appears condescending.

Intervene during report-back stages (except to keep time)   Tempting as it can be to intervene with reactions and comments, it is best to let report-back episodes flow. Jot down the things you would like to say, and have your say at an appropriate time, when the report-back stages have been completed.

Turn a discussion into an argument   Arguments can be valuable learning experiences if they are orchestrated in a skilled way—and when the people arguing are doing so knowingly and intentionally.

Things NOT to do! (contd)

However, spontaneous arguments often leave people feeling hurt or antagonistic. So, turning arguments into discussions is part of good facilitation, but not the reverse.

Get rattled!   Unless you are a very skilled actor.

81 A rattling good checklist!

This is a self-preservation device—but don't take it too seriously. It is intended for use on those occasions when you get 'rattled'. It is based on a workshop feedback questionnaire, but this time it is one for you to fill in.

Personal workshop feedback

You can do this during—or after—a less-than-happy workshop.

General views

I personally found the participants (put ticks at an appropriate distance from the various words—keeping your distance from any participants while doing this):

Stimulating	Boring
Useless	Useful
Relevant	Irrelevant
Rigid	Flexible
Well conducted	Poorly conducted
Demanding	Undemanding
Patronizing	Challenging
Too spread out	Too condensed
Coherent	Fragmented
Focused on my expertise	Focused on their prejudices
Worth my time spent	Not worth my time spent

Specific feedback

The two most useful participants at this workshop (besides myself) were:

-
-

The two least useful participants at the workshop were:

•

•

The thing that pleased me most about the way I ran the workshop was:

•

The thing that annoyed me most about the way the participants behaved was:

•

82 Breaks in breaks

Breaks are usually planned into workshops at mealtimes or coffee/tea times. Some of us really need time to ourselves, and become very unreceptive, possibly antisocial and even hostile if we are not able to spend some time alone with our own thoughts! It is easy to go on working through breaks, in fact it is often participants who keep the pace up and either follow up group work or pin down the facilitator. Beware of these individuals. Ways of planning for breaks in breaks include:

- Have quiet times built into programmes when people can hide alone if they wish, perhaps with tasks like reading, writing or thinking.
- Expect facilitators to have some time to themselves, not always to be available. Make it clear when you are and are not available, especially on residential courses.
- Be careful if the mood seems to become rather over-excited. Energy can be a disadvantage if people make reckless decisions (like the group who went midnight swimming in a cold and rough sea), so beware of developing high levels of energy and not using it all up in the workshop. If surplus energies seem to abound it is worth using them to do some forward planning or deliberate reflection rather than letting participants disperse too excited!
- Be aware of social processes in break times. Participants' moods and expectations can change dramatically during a break, as they discuss things informally with each other. Changes in their expectations can have an effect on the next part of the workshop, so be aware of what is happening during the breaks, and prepare to deal with any outcomes.
- Sometimes an unplanned break can revive and refresh—five minutes in fresh air is worth a lot.
- In long residentials it can be helpful to timetable 'walk/read/sleep' time during the day—perhaps after lunch in the siesta time!
- Consider using the environment if the workshop has an interesting location—water, trees and mountains can have very soothing effects.
- Physical exercise is essential to some, welcome to others. Allow time to use whatever facilities are available nearby.

Happy participants will not be longing for the next break because they will know when it is planned and will have some control over how they spend their personal time.

We remember being miserable in workshops when

- We needed a comfort break
- We wanted to make a phone call
- We wanted to explore new surroundings
- Outside looked more interesting than inside
- We wanted half an hour alone to lie down and think
- We wanted to unpack and have a shower having just arrived after a long journey
- We wanted to breathe some fresh air
- We wanted to feel the sun which had just come out after days of greyness
- We wanted to read the notes so far and digest some of the information
- We wanted to consider the implications of a new idea or a challenge to previous ones
- We wanted to get away from other people for a short time

All of these are distractions to learning which can be alleviated if workshops have reliable, frequent and publicly timetabled breaks.

83 Post-it lists to escape from jams

Sometimes you are floored! Something comes up that you just haven't thought about—or you suddenly realize that you have got 17 minutes before the lunch-break, and the next scheduled task cannot possibly be done in less than 30 minutes. It is on occasions like these that a pad of Post-its can be worth its weight in gold.

The unexpected question

Someone asks a dangerous question. There's an expectant silence. You know that if *you* answer the question, you will alienate at least half of the participants—or maybe you just don't have an answer to the question. Bring out the Post-its! Repeat the question—or write it on a flipchart. Ask everyone to write their own personal answer (or view) on a Post-it, and stick the Post-it (anonymously) on the wall—or on the flipchart. You can then spend a few minutes helping establish the overall response of those present. Even people with strong, minority views will feel better if their view has been considered, and is 'visible' to all.

Seventeen minutes to fill!

When a 'gap' comes up unexpectedly, it is always handy to have something useful to fill the time. Think back to any matters arising from the workshop so far, which have not been fully aired. Turn one of them into a question or proposal, write it on the flipchart, then give out the Post-its. Ask everyone to jot down their personal view or answer, and post it (anonymously) on the flipchart.

Any questions?

This is another way of dealing with that 17 minutes. If you were to ask 'any questions?' out loud, however, either there would be none (very embarrassing!) or there would be some that would take far more than 17 minutes to deal with. Give everyone a Post-it instead, and ask people to write their own questions down. Then stick them all on a flipchart, and choose which ones you wish to deal with at the present time, and which ones will be dealt with as the workshop unfolds later. With a bit of practice, this whole operation takes exactly 17 minutes, of course!

84 Dangers of debriefs

When participants (or syndicates) are reporting back to the whole work-shop group, there are undesirable consequences which may result, such as repetition, or one participant (or group) going on for too long.

The following possibilities help avoid the risk of a long series of lengthy, repetitive debriefs.

Establish ground-rules—especially regarding timing   It can be useful to agree, for example, that each syndicate will report back for up to six (say) minutes, with a further four (say) minutes for plenary discussion of matters arising. A kitchen timer can then be used to bleep at the appropriate intervals, with the general understanding (ground-rule) that anyone speaking at the time immediately gives way to the next phase of the debrief.

Establish a debrief format   For example, if individuals or syndicates have each been asked to prepare one flipchart (or one overhead trans-parency) as an aid to their debrief, it can be agreed that during the debrief, nothing will be 'read out' to the group that the group can't read for themselves from the flipchart or screen. Therefore, debriefs take the form of explanations and elaborations, rather than straight presentations.

Agree to avoid duplication   If several groups (or individuals) are reporting back on the same task, it can be agreed that successive debriefs only give additional or different points from those already given in earlier debriefs. (This also helps everyone awaiting their turn to debrief to pay greater attention to the successive debriefs.)

Set different tasks in the first place   When each debrief is reporting on a different task (or different aspect of a central task) there is far less probability of a series of repetitive debriefs. The order of the respective debriefs may, however, have to be chosen with some care.

85 Pooling contributions

If the session has resulted in some sort of output there are lots of ways in which the results can be shared. For example, if the session has been a discussion, syndicate activity or personal thinking:

- Each person or group could write their edited highlights on a flipchart sheet and either take turns to talk through it or present it to everyone else.
- Write on flipchart sheets but then stick these on the wall to be visited by everyone else.
- Write the flipcharts but then put them on chairs in a circle to be visited by everyone walking around the circle.
- Each person in turn holds up their contribution and takes questions on it.
- Each person puts their contribution on the wall behind them or at their feet on the floor.
- Each person or group reports back using an OHP transparency they have prepared. These can then be pasted to a flipchart and posted on the wall.

These can be developed into more formal presentations with prepared visual aids or exhibitions of products, depending on the time available, size of the group and nature of the activity. If the activity has involved making something rather than a discussion, the products themselves could lead to a discussion of the making process and the outcomes.

86 Support pairs

This is an idea for the end of a workshop. It is designed to re-stimulate the participants' intentions some weeks after the workshop is over.

Ask the participants to find a partner and then work out with their partners:

- What they want to achieve as a result of what they have learned at the workshop.
- What they may be able to do better as a pair than either might have done alone.
- What actions would move them towards what they want to achieve.
- When they intend to take each of the actions.

Explain the dangers that the plans they now have could wind up as simply 'good intentions' unless they take steps to prevent this.

Suggest that they arrange either to meet or telephone each other in one month's time to find out how successful the actions have been. Allow five minutes for the participants to sort out the arrangements for their post-workshop meeting or link-up (time, place, etc.).

87 Adding your own contribution

When groups or individuals are feeding back their discussion results, lists of points or comments about something, we often want to add our own points. The difficulty with this is that it can seem that the facilitator knew it all before and the whole exercise was a guessing game to try to match the hidden list.

Some ways to avoid this are:

Offer your own points before setting up discussion groups This has the disadvantage of still seeming to 'tell' everything that is necessary unless the subject area is wide and available to everybody.

Give two contradictory points of view, claiming neither This has the advantage that the facilitator can set off groups to discuss the viewpoints and report back, then additions can be from both viewpoints to supplement what the participants have worked out for themselves.

Give participants full information, maybe before the workshop This enables everyone to start from the same degree of information. The exercise will then need to be about using that information in some way.

Work from the participants' viewpoint Use questions such as 'What will you need to find out in order to . . . ' 'What do we already know about . . . ' 'How can we find out about . . . '

Give exercises that will come up with different results An example is to give each group a different topic or situation to discuss and have them report back in a way that reveals the common thread. This allows wide discussion of material in terms of best approach, options, could different ideas be linked, etc. The facilitator can encourage wide discussion and prod participants to add missing ideas.

88 Co-facilitating

Facilitating with another person is likely to be less stressful than facilitating alone. You have someone else to share workshop tasks such as the preparation and organization. You have someone with different perspectives and different abilities than your own to add to your awareness of developing situations in the workshop and different ideas of how to respond to them. You have someone to act as a sounding board to check out your perceptions of what is going on and how to handle it. Clearly the amount of facilitation skill and resources available to the group is greater with two people.

There are various ways that two (or more) people can co-facilitate. One approach is to decide for each workshop activity that one of you will be the 'lead' and the other will be the 'support'. If you do this then it is worth discussing at the outset what you actually mean by 'leading' and 'supporting'. For example, if you are the 'lead', what sort of (and how much) intervention do you want from the 'support'?

A second approach is for one person to be the facilitator proper and the other to be the observer. The observer can feed back their reflections to the facilitator whenever appropriate. The observer can note down significant verbatim comments made by participants to feed back to the group in plenary and review sessions.

The second person can act as trouble-shooter for handling difficulties that individual participants are experiencing which do not impact on the rest of the group (e.g., the departure of a participant from the workshop whose child has become ill). The second person can act as scribe for activities that require flipchart recording. For example, it is much easier to facilitate an effective brainstorm if someone else is recording the ideas. One person can give the instructions for a syndicate activity and the other can write them up.

Another type of division of labour is for one person to focus on content issues and for the other to focus on process issues. For example, in a plenary discussion, one facilitator takes primary responsibility for the intellectual content and the other takes primary responsibility for the other things that are happening within the group. This might include recognizing the person who is trying without success to get into the discussion, the person whose twitching foot indicates feelings of irritation, the fact that the session has overrun into scheduled lunch-time and so on.

Having a second facilitator enlarges the range of possible workshop activities. For instance, it would allow the group to divide into two halves for a particular activity where it would be useful for each half to have a facilitator around. When you are reviewing the workshop afterwards you have someone else to contribute a different perspective.

Another advantage of co-facilitating is that it can be a good way for someone to gain experience of facilitating groups.

89 I learned

Here is a way that you can use to bring new learning into conscious awareness. You can also use it to provide a summary phase of reflection at the end of any experiential exercise.

Prepare a chart with the following (or similar) sentence stems:

'I learned that I . . . '
'I realized that I . . .'
'I relearned that I . . . '
'I was surprised that I . . . '
'I noticed that I . . . '
'I discovered that I . . . '
'I was surprised that I . . . '
'I was pleased that I . . . '
'I was displeased that I . . . '

Give the participants a minute to reflect on what they learned from the activity about themselves or their values. Then ask them to use any one of the sentence stems to share with the group one or more of their feelings.

Don't call individual participants to contribute but ask them to volunteer whenever they feel comfortable to do so. Reassure them that they have the right to pass without saying anything.

You may want to ask the participants to write down a few 'I learned' statements before sharing them aloud. And you may also want to share some of your own. Don't allow discussion to interrupt the flow of the 'I learned' statements. Discourage participants from attempting to explain or defend their statements. Try to help the participants focus on personal learning rather than on generalities. Encourage the participants to 'own' their statements. Instead of saying 'I learned that people . . . ' say 'I learned that I . . . ' An alternative way of running the exercise is to form small groups of about four participants for sharing the 'I learned' statements (rather than sharing in full plenary with all the participants).

90 Re-planning the workshop

Elsewhere in the book we have looked at ideas on getting feedback from participants *during* a workshop, so that the workshop can be improved as it progresses. Here, we will look at a way of doing your own analysis of a workshop *after* the event, so that you can improve future workshops.

What worked well?

Schedule time to examine what worked well and what worked less well. This is a kind of 'review and reflect' session for the facilitator(s). The key question is 'With hindsight, what would I have done differently?' Answering this question is important—it is the key to how you can learn to run better workshops. Here is your opportunity to use the experiential learning cycle—experience, reflection, conceptualization and experimentation—to your own advantage. It is clear what is involved in having the experience of running the workshop and reflecting on it. It is less clear how to complete the learning cycle by 'conceptualization' and 'experimentation'. Our answer is to re-plan the workshop. This requires that you be very clear about what you would have done differently (conceptualization). It means that you have set up the conditions necessary to test out (experiment) a new (revised) workshop design the next time that you run a workshop on a similar theme. So in your workshop folder the last document to be inserted is one headed: 'Revised workshop following re-planning session'.

When should it be done?

When is the best time to do this? As soon as possible after the workshop—while you can still remember how you felt during each of the workshop activities and the thoughts and ideas that passed through your head during each of the activities. However, we find even the most exhilarating workshop exhausting. By the time that you have cleared up at the end of the workshop you probably won't have the energy to engage in an action replay of the event. If you are like us you will probably want to relax. So you may want to schedule an hour or two the morning after the workshop to re-plan it. At that time we have still got lots of energy for the workshop and we can remember what it was like. A week or two later and the energy levels have fallen as the workshop becomes 'water under the bridge' and it is difficult to bring to mind the incidents, thoughts and feelings of the workshop.

There is, of course, another advantage to all this: it means that when you come to design a workshop on a similar theme you already have a 'state of the art' plan to work from—a plan that embodies your learning from the last time that you ran it. We find it important to put the 'review and reflect' session in our diaries when we are designing the workshop, otherwise it gets squeezed out. Workshops tend to get planned and designed months in advance when diaries are fairly uncongested and it is relatively easy to find an hour or two after the workshop. By the time of the workshop, finding a slot in the diary immediately after the workshop is usually impossible. On longer workshops (residentials) we find it useful to have a daily 'review and reflect' period at the end of the afternoon session for the participants to process the workshop activities. And we use that period to 'review and reflect' on the day's activities and processes. We note the 'lessons' in a journal and this provides the basis of the post-workshop re-planning session.

91 Saying goodbye

Just as individual sessions need a sense of closure so does the whole workshop. Any of the following three activities gives all the participants an opportunity to share with the others some of the significance of the workshop to them.

What did you learn?

- Ask the participants to spend a minute thinking of one or two learning points from the workshop that are important to them and actions that they plan to take as a result of being at the workshop.
- Ask for a volunteer to share with the rest of the participants either a significant learning point or an action that they propose to do as a result of being at the workshop.
- Explain that after someone has shared their learning or action point then you will proceed clockwise (or anticlockwise, it doesn't matter so long as the participants know) around the group to give everyone an opportunity to share.
- Tell them that if there is nothing that they want to share then it is OK to say 'pass'.
- On a longer workshop this activity can be linked to the 'learning log'. If you have asked the participants to keep a learning log you can ask them to bring it to this last session and select something from the log to share with the other participants.
- Instead of offering the choice of a learning or an action point you could choose one or the other. If you have done a few rounds of 'learning points' already (this is only likely on a longer workshop) then it is probably best to focus on action points in this last round.

How did the workshop measure up?

This enables the participants to check out their aspirations for the workshop with what they actually gained from the experience.

Remind participants of their personal aims for the workshop that they stated at the beginning. They (or you) may have written these on flipcharts or Post-its or OHP acetates at the start of the workshop. Ask them to spend a minute reviewing the aims that they expressed or wrote when they arrived and then compare them with what they actually gained from the workshop.

Each participant (starting with yourself as facilitator) completes the following sentences:

'My main aim in attending the workshop was . . . '
'What I gained was . . . '

Avoid any discussion and don't seek explanations. If someone doesn't wish to contribute to this don't press them.

Appreciation and regrets

This is another 'round' designed to achieve a sense of closure at a workshop. This enables participants to express what they appreciate about the workshop and their regrets.

- Explain that the workshop will end with a round to enable participants to express what they appreciate and regret about the workshop. Let them know that you will be asking for someone to volunteer an 'appreciation and a regret' about the workshop.
- Pass sequentially round the room (specify whether this will be clockwise or anticlockwise) for contributions from other participants . . . 'and it's OK to pass when it comes to your turn if you want to'.
- Ask the participants to spend a minute thinking about what they appreciate and regret about the workshop. Let them know that it is OK to jot down any notes that help.
- After the minute ask for a volunteer and start the process. Don't forget to include yourself in the round.
- Sometimes the regrets are 'negative' (e.g. 'I came to the workshop hoping that we would have more lecture input; I regret that we didn't'). Often, however, the 'regrets' of participants will express positive reactions to the workshop (e.g. 'I regret that the workshop has come to an end as I've had such a good time and learned so much').
- As an alternative to the one minute's solitary reflection, ask the participants to spend three minutes talking with a partner about what they appreciate and regret about the workshop.
- Another alternative: after explaining about the 'rules' of the 'appreciate and regret' round, do a review of the activities of the workshop. This can help to remind participants about the experiences that they have had on the workshop.

92 Saying goodbye at a long workshop

This idea is for residential workshops that last more than a couple of days. It helps to acknowledge the identity and presence of the participants as individuals apart from their role as workshop participants.

Over the course of the residential make a note of 'incidents' involving the participants that occur outside of the workshop activities. The incidents can be pretty small. For example, 'When we arrived John discovered that the hotel key that he had been given didn't fit the door of his room . . . he thought he might have to spend the residential sleeping in the hotel foyer'.

You need to find an incident for all of the participants—some incidents may involve several participants (such as when 'Sally, David and Anne ordered frogs' legs as an experiment at dinner on the second night . . . and went to bed very hungry').

To end the workshop, you review the activities that the participants have undertaken on a day-by-day basis spicing it up with the personal incidents that you have recorded. This ensures that everyone's interest in the review is held as they wait to see if they are going to be mentioned and then feel satisfied that they have been noticed after they have been mentioned.

Our experience is that any residential that lasts three days or more will generate at least one incident for each participant for groups of up to about 20. If you are really pushed, then it is better to include a few incidents from the workshop sessions rather than exclude someone.

You need to be vigilant in recording the 'incidents'. We find that it is easy if you record them as you go along but it is very difficult to recall them at the end of a workshop. One way to ensure that you don't forget is to have an 'incidents notebook' which is your first priority to complete during breaks in the workshop.

93 Feedback: a simple questionnaire

Elsewhere in this book we have noted the dangers of using questionnaires for getting feedback from participants. If you are going to use them you might as well use them in a way that will help the participants do some learning along the way. Figure 93.1 is a questionnaire that we have sometimes used.

FEEDBACK TO THE FACILITATORS

We would be very grateful for your feedback. Please complete this sheet and return it at the end of the workshop. Thanks.

The three most helpful things that I learned at the workshop:

-
-
-

What I liked best about the workshop:

-

What I would have liked to have been different/recommendations for future workshops:

Any other comments on the workshop? (please continue overleaf if there is not enough room)

Name (optional): ....

Figure 93.1 *A simple questionnaire for obtaining feedback*

94 The dangers of questionnaires

Questionnaires can yield a lot of feedback in a short time, and can have the advantages of anonymity for participants wishing to express critical views. However, there are limitations on the value of questionnaire feedback.

WORKSHOP FEEDBACK						
Title of workshop:_____						
General views: I personally found the workshop: (please tick boxes)						
Stimulating						Boring
Useless						Useful
Relevant						Irrelevant
Plenty of discussion						Too little discussion
Rigid						Flexible
Well conducted						Poorly conducted
Demanding						Undemanding
Patronizing						Challenging
Too spread out						Too condensed
Coherent						Fragmented
Focused on my needs						Focused on tutor's opinions
Objectives achieved						Objectives not achieved
Little activity						Plenty of activity
Worth time spent						Not worth time spent

Figure 94.1 *Questionnaire enabling quick analysis*

Feedback from the sort of questionnaire shown in Fig. 94.1 can be analysed quickly—even statistically. The number of times a tick is made in each box can be summarized on a master-sheet. Note that sometimes 'good' things are on the left, and at other times on the right—this helps to avoid participants making one decision, then running down the form on the same basis. But read on for the dangers . . .

Some limitations of questionnaires

Because it is easy to administer, the questionnaire has become the dominant method of seeking feedback. Unfortunately, it is also easy to fall into the temptation to produce statistics based on questionnaire responses. If 84 per cent of participants think Mrs Smith's workshops are brilliant, we are inclined to ignore the 16 per cent who don't—THEY may have very good reasons for disliking her workshops. The problem is not so much with gathering feedback by questionnaire, but with the ways feedback is processed and collated.

The 'ticky-box' syndrome

People become conditioned to make instant responses to questions. Getting through the questionnaire quickly becomes a virtue! Responses are made on a surface level of thinking rather than as a result of reflection and critical thinking. (This is all right where 'instant' reaction is what is wanted, but the feedback is not usually analysed on that basis.)

'Performing dogs' syndrome

Many people filling in questionnaires tend to want to please! They can usually tell which responses will please the people giving them the questionnaire, and the people whose work is involved in the issues covered by the questionnaire. If they like the people, they are likely to comment favourably on things!

Lost learning opportunities

Questionnaires are often used after the event rather than during it. People don't then feel that the things they write on to the questionnaires will make any direct difference—at least as far as they themselves are concerned. The sense of ownership is reduced.

The 'wysiwyg' syndrome

(What you see is what you get.) Questionnaires produce feedback on the particular issues covered—but often NOT on other important issues. There is a tendency to design questionnaires that will give positive feedback!

'Blue, rosy and purple' questionnaires

A major limitation of most questionnaires is that responses are coloured by how people FEEL at the moment of filling them in. If the same questionnaire were used a few days later, some responses may be completely different! Yet the results are often statistically analysed as though they reflected 'permanent' reactions to questions and issues, rather than fleeting, transient reactions.

95 Substitutes for evaluation

'Workshop evaluation' is a term that is often used—but an activity that is seldom achieved. Real 'evaluation' of a workshop would involve follow-up over a period of months—even years—determining the nature of the real outcomes of the workshop. Nevertheless, there are several things that can be done to gain some measures of the effectiveness of a workshop.

Workshop feedback

This can be gathered orally at the end of the workshop, or by questionnaires administered at the end of the workshop, or shortly after the workshop. Despite the dangers associated with questionnaires mentioned in the previous item, they still provide useful information. A combination of 'structured' feedback and 'open-ended' feedback proves most useful. Examples of questionnaires attempting to gain both kinds of feedback are given in Figs. 95.1 and 95.2.

The 'ticky-box' page

The evidence produced by the sort of questionnaire shown in Fig. 95.1 on page 186 reflects participants' feelings at the end of the workshop, and does not necessarily give an accurate indication of the real value or quality of the workshop. (The worth of some 'excellent' workshops only 'dawns' gradually!) However, this feedback is very useful if you are going to be running a similar workshop quite soon with a new batch of participants—or if you are going to run further different workshops with the same batch of participants.

It is worth the few minutes making a 'master-sheet' summarizing all participants' entries on the grid. Where all the 'crosses' coincide in position, you have probably got a fairly accurate indication of how the workshop 'fared' on the dimension concerned. Where the crosses are spread out along a horizontal dimension, you have evidence that different participants felt differently about that particular aspect of the workshop.

Open-ended feedback

The page of open questions (Fig. 95.2 on page 187) can give really useful information. It is well worth separating the questions on 'usefulness' and 'pleasure/annoyance'.

WORKSHOP FEEDBACK

Title of workshop: ....

General views: I personally found the workshop: (please place crosses at appropriate positions on the 'scales' below)

                      'very' 'quite' ? 'quite' 'very'

Stimulating	Boring
Useless	Useful
Relevant	Irrelevant
Good discussion	Limited discussion
Rigid	Flexible
Well conducted	Poorly conducted
Demanding	Undemanding
Patronizing	Challenging
Spread out	Condensed
Coherent	Fragmented
Objectives achieved	Objectives not achieved
Good level of activity	Poor level of activity
Good use of time spent	Poor use of time spent

Figure 95.1   *A 'ticky-box' style of questionnaire*

Other evaluation approaches

The following are some of many possibilities for building up facets of the true 'evaluation' of a workshop.

A follow-up telephone 'round'

For example, conduct a series of 'telephone interviews' with the people who took part in the workshop, using a checklist of questions. Write down key phrases from the replies from each participant. Remember to ask some 'open' questions, to ensure that you gather feedback that goes beyond the scope of your list of questions. Telephone follow-up tends

The two most useful elements of the workshop were:

-
-

The two least useful elements of the workshop were:

-
-

The thing that pleased me most about the way the workshop was run was:

-

The thing that annoyed me most about the way the workshop was run was:

-

The workshop helped me personally as follows:

-

Any other comments, criticisms, or suggestions:

(Thanks for your feedback—it is highly valued)

Figure 95.2   An open-ended questionnaire

to be more useful than a follow-up questionnaire—you can expect a 'biased' response to such questionnaires; i.e. only those who were highly pleased, or highly displeased, tend to reply.

A follow-up interview with the 'client'

Often, it is worth asking the supervisors or managers of the participants what sort of developments have taken place since the workshop. These people will probably have received feedback about the workshop too.

Keep track of 'word-of-mouth' recommendations

When you are asked to do similar workshops in the future, it will often be on the basis of someone having 'spoken glowingly' of a workshop you conducted previously. Try to work out what caused that person to have a high opinion of the workshop, and build on the causes in future workshops.

Keep in touch with past participants

Make sure you have lists of names and addresses, so that if something new comes up (e.g. a new discussion paper you write), you can send it to people who have attended your workshops. You will often get replies containing additional feedback and 'evaluative comments'.

96 Have a moan session

If there is an undercurrent of 'whingeing' it can work best to acknowledge it rather than to ignore it, to bring it out into the open and try to deal with it.

Some possible ways include:

- Individuals in pairs tell each other their personal moans and they discuss them. Then they try to come up with ways of improving the situation. Each pair then presents their moans and solutions to the whole group.
- The group brainstorms all moans without discussion then goes through the list sorting out important issues from the ones that do not really matter. The whole group then looks for solutions to the important moans.
- As above, but in small groups which report back to the whole group.
- Anonymous moans are written on paper and put in a box. The facilitator puts all of these on a flipchart and everyone writes a solution to each moan. The solutions are then also written up, and the moans and solutions are discussed.
- Anonymous moans are written on Post-it slips and stuck onto a flipchart. The facilitator groups the moans into related themes. The group can then write solutions on different coloured Post-it slips and put these with each cluster of moans for discussion and comment.

For a session like this to really address the issues it is necessary to be prepared to act on the proposed solutions as far as possible or to carry them to whatever forum has the power to act.

97 Workshop products

One of the main differences between a workshop and more didactic forms of the teaching–learning situation is that during a workshop participants should have developed or discovered things themselves. They should have invented answers to questions, clarified issues, discovered matters arising, even re-invented wheels. At a good workshop participants will have developed a feeling of ownership of the steps they made. These are some of the 'products' of a workshop.

At the end of the workshop, participants will often have a considerable degree of enthusiasm for the things they did during the workshop, the tasks they tackled, and the discussions they engaged in. Two weeks later, however, the workshop is likely to have faded in their minds, and details of the conclusions they came to may be fading. Even if they have handout material to remind them of the content of the workshop, the more intimate side of the things they themselves did may be beginning to evaporate.

One way of helping participants retain their own personal thoughts is to record principal stages of the workshop in a 'workshop products' collection and issue the collected products of the workshop to each participant (by post if participants are dispersed). The exact nature of the workshop products will vary depending on the nature of the workshop and the number of participants, but there are some general principles that can be applied to assembling the workshop products. For example, it is often useful to do the following:

- Transcribe participants' expectations, especially if these were gathered with their individual names attached.
- Transcribe the products of syndicate activities, e.g. when syndicates reported back using an overhead transparency as a vehicle to convey their findings.
- Transcribe the principal flipcharts built up during group discussions or brainstorms.
- Assemble together the results of Post-it activities, grouping the products in a coherent and logical manner.
- Include a copy of the workshop aims or objectives.
- Include any paperwork showing the outline programme, to remind participants of the structure of the workshop.
- Include an analysis of the feedback obtained from participants, especially individual remarks (congratulatory or otherwise).

- If the workshop included action planning, transcribe the action plans, possibly adding comments and suggestions during the process of transcribing them.

Much of the task of building up workshop products is routine transcription—this can be done by someone who was not even present at the event itself. When transcribing, it is important to transcribe and not transmute. Participants often remember the exact phrase they used—this is what they need to see in the workshop products if they are to get a real sense of ownership of the workshop findings. However, it is often tempting to respond to some of the ideas generated by participants (or reply to some of their feedback comments) and such responses can easily be added. It needs to be clear which parts are responses; this can be achieved by making all responses conform to a particular style (e.g. by using brackets, italics, a particular print font, a particular print size, and so on).

We have found that it usually takes a time equivalent to half the workshop duration to assemble a full report of the workshop. The task can be accelerated if photocopies of original workshop acetates and flipcharts can be made—though the credibility of the products of the workshop is often enhanced by using desk-top publishing and creating a professional-looking collection based on participants' products.

The ideal time for participants to receive workshop products is usually just after the workshop! However, a time lapse of a few days is acceptable—maybe in some cases desirable, e.g. when it is advantageous for participants to have had some time to reflect on issues that arose during the workshop.

98 Action planning

One positive way of ending a workshop is to plan how to use what has been learnt in the future. There are lots of ways we have done this:

- Ask people to spend a few minutes individually, thinking of how they could use what they have learnt, then to write down some of these ways, preferably with details of exactly when, how, who with, etc.
- Spend time in pairs after a first, short, personal thinking time and have pairs help each other to set detailed objectives.
- Ask groups to flipchart what they have learnt and to discuss how this can be used in future. Gather feedback in a plenary session and flipchart the participants' ideas regarding ways to put their learning into practice.
- If groups have worked closely together they can help each other to set objectives and make commitments to the group to feedback results. This is good if there is to be another workshop after a break.
- Produce forms for people to write their action plans—with spaces for what has been learnt, how it can be applied, why, when and where, maybe a schedule and a contract to sign with someone else to help keep it under review.
- Some groups like to form self-help networks, to share addresses and phone numbers and keep in touch over developments.

Personal action plan

It can help to have a format for action planning. A personal form for each individual can be devised to help them to sort out what they will do as a result of the workshop. Sections should include:

- A description of targets or goals
- What action is needed to get there
- Exactly what will be counted as success
- Target dates for actions and for completion

It can also help to have someone to act as a reviewer, to get in touch on agreed review dates—another way in which pairing can be helpful. A sample form is shown in Fig. 98.1. It can be useful to ask participants to sign and date each others' action plans after they have discussed them.

Personal action plan

In the light of your thinking and activities during this workshop, what are now your principal related targets or goals? Write the top three in order of priority:

1

2

3

What actions will be necessary for you to achieve these targets?

      Your actions   Other people's actions

1

2

3

For each of your three main targets, write below something that would be visible evidence that you had achieved your target:

1

2

3

Target dates: please enter three dates below, and alongside them indicate which actions you plan to have completed by these dates, or which targets you will have achieved by these dates:

1

2

3

Date:.................. Name:...

Contact address or phone number: ....

....

Figure 98.1 *A personal action plan*

99 Taking care of yourself

One of the best things that you can do to ensure the success of your workshop is to take care of yourself. A haggard, stressed facilitator is unlikely to provide a workshop experience that is either enjoyable or productive for the participants.

Being prepared

One thing that you can do to minimize the stress of running your workshop is to be as prepared as you reasonably can be. It is helpful to try to hold your awareness on the experience of the workshop participants. If you are not prepared, then coping with last minute difficulties will divert your attention from this focus.

There are several ways in which a little pre-workshop attention will pay dividends.

Arrive early for the workshop

This will enable you to sort out the seating arrangements and check arrangements with the venue (times of refreshments, lunch, etc.). Turning up with only a few minutes to go and finding that the seats are arranged in rows as opposed to the circle of chairs that you wanted gives you little time to do anything except panic.

Check out the equipment beforehand

Make sure that you know what you will do if the equipment fails. If you are going to use OHPs make sure that you have two spare bulbs. In general the higher the level of the technology that you intend to use the more hostages you give to fortune. If the video machine breaks down, it is better to have a contingency activity to move into than to spend time trying to repair it.

Take supplies

Take a supply of flipchart paper, flipchart pens, Blu-tack, etc., in case these are not provided at the venue where the workshop is located.

Conserve your energy

You don't have to spend time with the participants outside the workshop sessions. There may be occasions when you feel that it will be valuable in terms of developing rapport or getting feedback on how the workshop is going. On the other hand, you may find that 'being on parade' at all times uses up a great deal of your energy and you would rather spend some time revising the rest of the workshop programme in the light of the way that it has gone so far, or simply being on your own, recharging your batteries. You may also find that the sort of feedback that you get on these occasions is less valuable because friendly participants tell you what they think you want to hear. Whether, and how much, time you spend with them outside the workshop sessions is mostly a matter of your own personal style—you do have a choice.

Make a 'loading list'   This is a bit like a shopping list. When you have planned all you can for a workshop, sit down with the programme and make a list of all the things you need to have with you for it to work. Go through each time slot and examine what you will need to be using, adding things to your list. One of our loading lists is shown in Fig. 99.1.

Sat/Sun

Kit (check OHP pens and flip pens)
Player and CDs
Copies of pre-workshop notes sent out
Flipchart paper
Spares of programme notes and participants' lists
Handouts (green label box)
OHP transparencies
Blank acetates
Reference books and example packages
Straws. pins. lego (for team task)
Choc biks. bar money. diary
Hats for role-play
Jennie's notes to give back
Examples of projects

Figure 99.1   A loading list

If you run the same workshop often, it can save a lot of time to file your loading list along with the resources you use for that particular workshop.

100 Finally—keep thinking laterally

We would like to end this book with a couple of related ideas that can be used in all sorts of imaginative ways. Both concern lateral thinking, or transferring one frame of reference to another. You can build these things into your workshops, or you can enjoy them yourself as a way of exploring new possibilities to plan and run workshops. You can use them to develop new activities which allow participants to 'stretch their minds' or relax.

Mix a metaphor

Using a metaphor can help you to take a fresh look at a situation or a problem. As an example, here is a metaphor applied to a workshop.

Think of something that has some parallels with workshop situations—possibly factories, building sites, places where people were busy doing things together or alone. Really, of course, these are only different types of workshops. Think of ideas further away from the subject of workshops, involving other living things—animals, perhaps, in a circus or a zoo. Or think of plants growing—this can lead to the basic idea of a garden. This can be a useful metaphor.

Imagine you have become the owner of a garden.

What can you do with a garden?

- Watch it and see what happens
- Dig it all up and start fresh
- Explore it, weed it a bit, tidy up
- Prune a bit, let in some light, refresh it
- Add things, remove things, replace things
- Build walls and fences
- Make paths
- Reorganize, make new groups, move things around
- Grow a variety of flowers, vegetables, fruit
- Listen to the birds and bees
- Lie back in the sun and contemplate
- Encourage butterflies to watch

- Have a barbecue
- Frame the view, modify the view
-
-
-

You can probably think of lots more things you could do with a garden. Try to add a few more ideas of your own to this list without thinking about how any of it applies to workshops.

The next stage is to apply the metaphor to the real situation, to 'force-fit' the garden ideas to a workshop situation.

What can you do with a workshop?

Watch it and see what happens   This is a bit slow and risks not a lot happening—probably everyone would sit around asking who was going to organize them. You could set up things to do and watch how participants tackle tasks and personal relationships. You could then help them to review this themselves and to learn from their own behaviour.

Dig it all up and start fresh   You could assume that there is nothing there worth keeping and try to dig out all the out of date or inappropriate knowledge, attitudes, skills, etc. then try to replace them with your preferred version. This raises issues of handling 'unlearning', re-learning or re-training, training for prescribed behaviour, 'who knows best', how experience is valued, etc.

Explore it, weed it a bit, tidy up   Find out what knowledge, skills and attitudes are held and test them a little, explore their relevance and appropriateness to now. Encourage everyone to consider how up to date they are, what historical 'baggage' could be thrown away, what new areas of learning could be explored now.

Prune a bit, let in some light, refresh it   A bit like the previous point—reconsider long-term acquisitions of knowledge, skills or attitudes. Seek enlightenment through using new approaches; maybe explore unfamiliar ideas and techniques.

Add things, remove things, replace things   What can you add to enhance, broaden, add variety, interest, depth. Renew and replace, update. Help participants find out what they want to add, remove or replace. Ask them what they want to keep doing, stop doing, do more of or less of.

Build walls and fences   Explore how people have compartmentalized their knowledge and skills, how much they are able to transfer prior learning to different situations. Is it ever useful to have walls and fences around areas of learning? What causes these barriers? Can we remove them or avoid them if we want to? Can we make gates, doors, openings if barriers are too strong to remove?

Make paths   Create approaches to areas, stepping stones, routes. Acknowledge the need for ways into new areas of learning and look at how to make links from existing learning to new learning. Plan how people might approach new topics and activities and allow for emotional and attitudinal reactions to be examined, not suppressed.

Reorganize, make new groups, move things around   Make physical changes in how the room is organized, move furniture, equipment, focus points, who sits next to whom, which people work together. Change rooms, change chairs, sit on the floor, move tables out or in. Find different ways of forming groups, different ways of evaluating how groups work.

Grow a variety of flowers, vegetables, fruit   How can you help people grow? Is there a difference in 'growing' different types of learning? How can you make the ground fertile for learning? How can you encourage and protect the first fragile growth? How can you help the growth to strengthen and become independent of your nurturing? What are the flowers of learning? What are the fruits? What are the vegetables?

Listen to the birds and bees   Get back in touch with our senses. Rediscover what is always around us but we have learnt not to notice. Concentrate on listening. Try different types of listening and discover how well people are listening to each other and how they can improve listening skills. Distinguish listening from hearing and explore how we select and interpret from available information.

Lie back in the sun and contemplate   Allow time to think. Time to feel comfortable, bathed in warmth, basking, reflecting. Think beyond the here and now, float, daydream, imagine. Help people to go outside themselves, to visualize new and better situations. Use relaxation and visualization techniques.

Encourage butterflies to watch   Some ideas are very fragile, some people make very tentative contributions, sometimes these are not noticed and lost. Heighten awareness of this, encourage the group to notice and point out 'butterflies' and to enjoy, examine, use them more.

Have a barbecue   Sharing food with people adds a dimension to the relationship and can help to build trust and mutual understanding. Preparing and cooking food together increases this effect. Everybody has to eat sometime! Consider the arrangements for coffee and lunch breaks and whether you could make them contribute more to the workshop, add to the experience, further the purpose in some way.

Frame the view, modify the view   Views change as you move your position, things change their relationships with other things and people. Broad and narrow views, looking under and over obstacles, looking through things. People sometimes look through the same 'frame' at everything and see only a narrow picture, miss all the richness of the environment. Taking different standpoints, role play, case studies can help people to see things differently.

There are all sorts of further possibilities for the initial idea of a garden, such as making a pond, encouraging trees, building a sandpit, putting up a swing . . .

We shall leave it to you to work out how you could extend these to your workshops.

Analogies

Analogies provide a way of harnessing the creativity of workshop participants, and turning to their advantage their different perspectives and views. Analogies are particularly useful when you are running a workshop on a new development or innovation which may seem threatening or even alien to participants. Analogies can help them link the 'new' topic to things they are already accustomed to. In this case, in some ways the more 'way-out' the metaphor is, the more interesting can be the results.

For example, analogies were used at a workshop on 'Designing Self-help Networks'. Some of the participants were the sort of people who preferred to work independently, and therefore they needed 'warming up' to the general idea of the benefits of networking. Participants were asked to think of something triggered off in their imaginations by the term 'networks'. One workshop participant thought of 'Crewe station'.

In the next stage of the process, each participant was asked to develop the image they had thought of without any further thoughts about the original term 'networks'. They were asked to list features of their imaginary idea. For example 'Crewe station' had features such as:

- many tracks
- many connections possible
- some trains pass it by
- some trains are new and plush, others are old and dirty
- everyone regards punctuality as important
- some trains are electric, some are diesel
- a buffet on each main platform
- announcements
- television monitors

and so on.

The next stage is to ask participants to link the features they have thought of regarding their imagined images, using the original trigger-word, and then extract or develop ideas that relate to the original concept (in this case self-help networks). In this way, ideas for improving the functioning of the original concept can be worked out. For example, a self-help network is improved by 'announcements' (good communications) and 'punctuality' (everyone keeping to deadlines they agree upon).

Analogies can be introduced by asking participants to 'freewheel' in their minds regarding oddly-contrasted images, e.g.:

'How is a large group like a violin?'
'How is a wordprocessing system like a piece of sponge cake?'

and so on. As you can imagine, great fun can be had at workshops in using analogies—provided that the participants are reasonably convinced that it is going to be useful to them. We advise that you take care not to force analogies (or any other lateral-thinking technique) on to participants who wish to remain firmly objective and on-target.

101 Conclusion: cast your bread . . .

In this book we have shared everything we could think of on running workshops—we have 'cast our bread upon the waters'. We would like to end by encouraging you to do the same. As we mentioned in the introduction to the book, we will be delighted to include your ideas (with due reference, of course) in the next edition of this book. Simply write to any of us (care of the publishers).

Workshop tricks and wrinkles

(Top secret) We have met workshop facilitators who develop highly professional workshops, but who seem very wary to give away their experience and techniques (despite the fact that workshops are 'public' occasions anyway). We can understand this, but it is perhaps not a very happy position. While it may seem very tempting to polish up a particular workshop formula till it runs like clockwork every time, it can actually be quite depressing to go round the city (or country, or world) running the same old workshop—we all need an element of challenge and a whiff of the unknown to produce a magical workshop. While it sometimes makes business sense to jealously guard copyrights, documents, ideas and experience, it makes 'life sense' to keep moving on. One of the best ways of continuing to move on to new challenges is to enable other people to do the things you can already do, by passing on your bag of tricks.

What can you pass on? Certain components of a bag of tricks are easy enough to pass on to other people. These include:

- Workshop programmes and formats
- Activities, exercises
- Handouts, resources
- Processes, techniques
- Advice and experience

In other words, it is possible to 'cascade' your workshops, and enable other people to do what you have done. This book is our way of cascading our workshops.

What can't be passed on?

We have often been asked to run workshops, where the stated intention was that the participants would then cascade the workshop widely within their organization. Surprisingly often, we have been asked back to run repeat sessions instead. This got us thinking 'What did we not manage to pass on?' It seems to rest in the 'future conditional' tense—in other words, what we could not pass on is 'What we would have done next if . . . '. This, of course, is not surprising. Few workshop facilitators can tell you what they would do when the unexpected happened—not till after they have done it. Nor can we. It would seem that the more people know about how you run your workshops, the more they are interested in what you might have done if . . . In other words, you are probably getting yourself into more work when you share your tips and wrinkles.

So, we look forward to hearing from you. We hope our ideas are proving useful to you—and we hope to learn from your experience and to help to share it.

Your own notes and ideas

Your own notes and ideas

Bibliography and further reading

Relevant educational approaches and theories

Claxton, G. (1984) *Live and Learn: An Introduction to the Psychology of Growth and Change in Everyday Life*, London, Harper and Row.

Knowles, M. (1980) *The Modern Practice of Adult Education: From Psychology to Andragogy*, Chicago, Follet.

Knowles, M. (1984) *The Adult Learner: A Neglected Species*, 3rd edition, Texas, Gulf.

Kolb, D. (1984) *Experiential Learning: Experience as the Source of Learning and Development*, New Jersey, Prentice-Hall.

Rogers, C. (1984) *Freedom to Learn for the 1980s*, Ohio, Merrill.

Smith, R. (1984) *Learning How to Learn: Applied Theory for Adults*, Milton Keynes, Open University Press.

Other sources of workshop activities

Bond, T. (1986) *Games for Social and Life Skills*, London, Hutchinson.

Hart, L. (1989) *Saying Hello: Getting your Group Started*, Pennsylvania, Organization Design and Development Inc.

Hart, L. (1989) *Saying Goodbye: Ending a Group Experience*, Pennsylvania, Organization Design and Development Inc.

Jelfs, M. (1982) *Manual for Action: Techniques to Enable Groups Engaged in Action For Change to Increase Their Effectiveness*, London, Action Resources Group.

Jones, K. (1992) *Imaginative Events: A Sourcebook of Innovative Simulations, Exercises, Puzzles and Games*, Vols. 1 and 2, London, McGraw-Hill.

Newstrom, J., and Scannell, E. (1980) *Games Trainers Play*, New York, McGraw-Hill.

Pedler, M., Burgoyne, J., and Boydell, T. (1986) *A Manager's Guide to Self-Development*, 2nd edition, London, McGraw-Hill.

Pfeiffer, J. and Jones, J. (annual) *Handbook of Structured Experiences for Human Relations Training*, California, University Associates.

Rae, L. (1988) *50 Activities for Developing Management Skills*, Aldershot, Gower.

Schwab, J., Baldwin, M., Gerber, J., Gomori, M., and Satir, V. (1989) *The Satir Approach to Communication: A Workshop Leader's Manual*, California, Science and Behaviour Books.

Simon, S., Howe, L., and Kirschenbaum, H. (1978) *Values Clarification: A Handbook of Practical Strategies for Teachers and Students*, New York, Dodd, Mead and Co.

Woodcock, M. (1989) *50 Activities for Teambuilding*, Aldershot, Gower.

Other useful material

Auvine, B., Densmore, B., Extrom, M., Poole, S., and Shanklin, M. (1977) *A Manual for Group Facilitators*, Wisconsin, Centre for Conflict Resolution.

Bolan, L. (1976) 'Group leader effectiveness', in *Developing Social Skills in Managers*, London, Macmillan.

Brookfield, S. (1986) *Understanding and Facilitating Adult Learning: A Comprehensive Guide to Principles and Effective Practices*, San Francisco, Jossey-Bass.

Clark, N. (1990) *Managing Personal Learning and Change*, London, McGraw-Hill.

Heron, J. (1990) *The Facilitators' Handbook*, London, Kogan Page.

Houston, G. (1984) *The Red Book of Groups and How to Lead Them Better*, Rochester Foundation.

Leigh, D. (1991) *A Practical Approach to Group Training*, London, Kogan Page.

Megginson, D., and Pedler, M. (1991) *Self-Development: A Facilitator's Guide*, London, McGraw-Hill.

Pont, T. (1990) *Developing Effective Training Skills*, London, McGraw-Hill.

Rae, L. (1983) *The Skills of Training*, Aldershot, Gower.

Randall, R., Southgate, J., and Tomlinson, F. (1980) *Cooperative and Community Group Dynamics*, London, Barefoot Books.

Rogers, J. (1977) *Adults Learning*, 2nd edition, Milton Keynes, Open University Press.

Keyword index

Note: We have not included in this index the themes that run throughout the book, such as 'activity', 'workshop planning', 'workshop processes', 'groupwork', 'facilitation' and so on, but we have tried to list the principal items under which you will find references to the following terms or processes.

Further titles in the McGraw-Hill Training Series

THE BUSINESS OF TRAINING
Achieving Success in Changing World Markets
Trevor Bentley   ISBN 0-07-707328-2

EVALUATING TRAINING EFFECTIVENESS
Translating Theory into Practice
Peter Bramley   ISBN 0-07-707331-2

DEVELOPING EFFECTIVE TRAINING SKILLS
Tony Pont   ISBN 0-07-707383-5

MAKING MANAGEMENT DEVELOPMENT WORK
Achieving Success in the Nineties
Charles Margerison   ISBN 0-07-707382-7

MANAGING PERSONAL LEARNING AND CHANGE
A Trainer's Guide
Neil Clark   ISBN 0-07-707344-4

HOW TO DESIGN EFFECTIVE TEXT-BASED OPEN
LEARNING:
A Modular Course
Nigel Harrison   ISBN 0-07-707355-X

HOW TO DESIGN EFFECTIVE COMPUTER-BASED
TRAINING:
A Modular Course
Nigel Harrison   ISBN 0-07-707354-1

HOW TO SUCCEED IN EMPLOYEE DEVELOPMENT
Moving from Vision to Results
Ed Moorby   ISBN 0-07-707459-9

USING VIDEO IN TRAINING AND EDUCATION
Ashly Pinnington   ISBN 0-07-707384-3

TRANSACTIONAL ANALYSIS FOR TRAINERS
Julie Hay   ISBN 0-07-707470-X

SELF-DEVELOPMENT
A Facilitator's Guide
Mike Pedler and
David Megginson   ISBN 0-07-707460-2

DEVELOPING WOMEN THROUGH TRAINING
A Practical Handbook
Liz Willis,
Jenny Daisley   ISBN 0-07-707566-8